Who Cares? I do.

By

Eno  Ikpe Anwana

# FOREWORD

This book is inspired by the voice of the Holy Spirit. Listen prayerfully to what the Lord is "saying to your heart" and not your head. Ask God to help you bring the message in this book alive in your soul as this is a sure help in time of need for this generation.

Some of us are lost in being able to relate with our children or understand them and the things happening within or around them but this book will cause you to have not just a glimpse but deep insight while also helping you know them better.

God knows you have been calling for answers and He is providing these answers in this book. He says in Jeremiah 33:3 *"call upon me, and I will answer thee, and show thee great and mighty things, which thou knowest not."*

This book is able to make you wise and as I went through the chapters of this book, I began to admire and appreciate the depth of knowledge and wisdom God has used the author to unfold; the question is "who will be privileged as I am to read this book?"

Reading *"Who cares, I do"*, being a pastor and preacher of the word, I felt like running to all parents and families to share my discovery, teaching them, hinting them, empowering them from the wisdom in this book. I began to pray earnestly that neither I nor my children and indeed this generation will be careless over our destinies in God.

Beloved, this is one book you cannot ignore. It is designed and packaged to make life simple and fulfilling. Chapters two and three are eye popping, mind blowing and very educative. It is bound to improve your relationship and communication with your children whilst also making you understand which point they are in their lives and how best to deal with it.

Wisdom is the principal thing and much wisdom is embedded in this book so my congratulations goes to you in advance as you come out empowered with the rarest of information.

**Pst (Mrs.) Eno Esenam**

Co- pastor, Church of God Mission Int'l , London

and Co-ordinator,Christian Women Fellowship Int'l (CWFI) London United Kingdom.

# ACKNOWLEDGEMENT

I would like to thank the following persons who have contributed immensely to the production of this book.

Worthy of mention are Pst.(Mrs.) Eno Esenam who wrote my foreword, Mrs Gloria Maculay, Mrs.Cecelia Kyari and Mrs. Emem Anwana, Ade Inubile, Bunmi Bello and Becky Odungide who all painstakingly proof read the book for me.

Thank you also to Mrs. Nandir Fred for her wonderful insights and the whole Glory House teenage /youth church for their slang contributions and interpretations.

I am also very grateful to my numerous friends, students, in different schools who introduced me to their world of youthful antics, fads and fears. Also to my staff at Finishing Touches and team members in ROC teens, Glory House.

Finally, many thanks to my husband Ikpe-Koko who has encouraged and supported me throughout the period of this work.

Without all your meaningful contributions, this book would never have been produced. This work is the product of our collective efforts, and above all, the grace of God.

## DEDICATION

*To my mother, for teaching me to love and care about others and to my three wonderful children-Kemek, Dara and Dase for letting me into their world of youthful fun and mischief.*

# ABOUT THE AUTHOR

Eno Anwana is a leadership teacher, conference speaker and the chief executive officer of Finishing Touches Corporation Ltd, an etiquette and corporate training firm based in London, United Kingdom. She is a mentor to several youths and also serves as a pastor and youth teacher in Glory House ministries, United Kingdom.

Eno has been committed to imparting the younger generation through her various youth workshops and programmes-"Manners Matter" and "Setapart". Her simple down-to-earth style, practical approach and a keen sense of humour endears people to her teaching.

She is also an ardent reader and researcher. She also holds a B.Sc in Marine Biology , an M.Sc in Aquaculture and a PGCE in Secondary Science. She is married and has three children.

# QUOTE

*"Train up a child in the way he should go , and when he is old he will not depart from it"*

......... King David   (Proverbs 22:5-7)

# CONTENTS

# Prologue

*"Grandma!! Grandma!!"*

Yelled my seven year old nephew from the bottom of the staircase, reluctant to go upstairs to relay the message given him by my uncle directly to my mother. There was dead silence at the other end.

*"Grandma! Are you there?"* he yelled again, still not wanting to move from where he was.

I was sure my mother was upstairs and unlike my nephew I understood what the silence from my mother meant. So I quietly watched with keen interest to see how this scene between my nephew and my mother will eventually play out.

Again, he attempted calling out to get an answer from her, not wanting to go upstairs so he wouldn't miss one minute of his favourite cartoon - The Simpsons.

Suddenly, I heard a door squeak and I looked up and saw my mother standing at the top of the staircase and her eyes said it all. Instantly, I knew my little nephew Don was in trouble.

*Don! She said firmly. "Where are your manners ? Come upstairs this moment!*

What transpired thereafter leaves much to the imagination........Hm ! I could never try that stunt while I was growing up or could you? Such offences were not taken lightly and it could cost you a fun activity or precious play time with your friends.

Centuries ago, manners reflected a lot about who you were and where you came from and to some extent who you might likely turnout to be(or so they said). Generally, people in the Western world were perceived as being well mannered, well groomed people who understood clearly the ethics of proper thought -out words, clear diction, sensible dating, proper dressing and courteous behaviour . How times have changed! Now the question seems to be *"Who cares ? "*

Good manners and etiquettes theoretically first came to me as a getaway for the summer holidays. My parents at the time were both undergraduate students at Howard University whilst working part-time. It was pertinent that my siblings and I had to have a lot of out of school hours care in order for them to find the balance between being students and parents. So we were placed in an after school club in Chillum Elementary School, Chillum Heights , Maryland where unknown to me at the time I was taught valuable skills for life. These teachings came in form of games, lectures, workshops and group projects and they formed the bedrock of the principles that has over the years guided my judgments severally from that tender age of seven till date. Suffice it to say that my parents were pleased that the classes were reinforcing core values they had been trying to teach me for years -only this time I listened.

That's where the journey for this book begins. I found myself caught within a cross- cultural web of very new daunting attitudes, outlandish style and out of this world slang language .

Also,my having an African background (where discipline is key) and now resident in the United Kingdom (where there are more liberal attitudes ), keeping the balance for my three children has become more of a monumental challenge to me than anything I've had to deal with in a long time. To many parents like me, raising kids to be well behaved , responsible, independent individuals in a fast-paced modern, technological society has proven to be quite daunting! However, it's a responsibility I feel parents owe to their children and to the society.

Raising children this century is not an easy hurdle as trends and times are continually changing. To be a great parent these days require a lot of tact, skills and common sense judgment. One must be up to speed with what the society speaks, accepts and values especially if you have to work or deal with young children. Suffice it to say most "acceptable" trends these days are quite irresponsible to say the least, but how many of us parents notice or really care? Well,I do and I'm sure if you're reading this book right now you must care too.

The above coupled with my passion for moral savvy and changing parental concerns inspired me to write this book *"Who cares ? I do"*. This book is intended to serve as a guide for parents ,young adults and others who have no choice but care about the growing change in attitude, acceptable behaviour and trends of the 21$^{st}$ century children and how to keep the balance everyday with them and society.

# Chapter One

## 21$^{st}$ Century Spoilers

*"Hey miss, that was crunk!"*

A youngster said to me one day as I was packing up to go after a class. I stood there feeling confused and watched as the young teenager sauntered out of the class. I turned to my class assistant who was there with me and asked ;

*"Was that good or bad? "*

And the young volunteer laughed, quickly understanding my dilemma and reassured me that the youngster was actually paying me a compliment and went further to interpret the whole gibberish as follows;

*"Hey miss, the class was awesome!"*

Bemused I sat down for a moment and heaved a sigh of relief, then it suddenly occurred to me that if I was to keep working with young adults I would have to learn this new language and attitudes fast.

So what is the new wave called? It's called Street!........

For the past years I have been carefully watching and learning the fast emerging trends and attitudes fizzle from the younger to older generations. Frankly, the younger 21$^{st}$st century bloomers seem to have gotten the older ones stripped of what use to be common sense, behaviour and manners. More often you would find parents adapting to speak the street slangs and even adopt the offensive attitudes usually only associated with teenagers.

I have tried to compile a few changing attitudes from different cultures, countries and generations that will expose a few of you to what I term as the 21$^{st}$ century spoilers.

*"Crump! You're a safa. Wanna cotch down my yard?*

If a teenager said the words (above) to you, should you be offended or flattered?

The answer, thankfully, is flattered, since a rough translation is ;

*"Wow! You are the coolest person. Do you want to hang out at my place?"*

Society is more geared than ever towards young people, but their slang - and the speed at which it changes – can be a mystery to those old enough to vote.

This coded language designed to exclude adults is being used more often than before and has become universally accepted to a wide range of youngsters worldwide.

So which words are current in the classroom now and on the streets? The main influences seem to be Creole Patois and rapper slangs treated in more detail in chapter two.

Ever walked down the street during summer and wondered, did I just see that? Well, you are not alone and often I wonder, did their parents not see them before they left home? Some of these kids are as young as 12years old. We need to wake up and see that the world is moving really fast! Children these days don't just need a watchful eye but need a firm - "pull up those trousers "attitude from parents too.

Dressed in a pair of Levi jeans hanging half way down his rump to reveal his checkered boxers, Jack struts down the pavement with his friends all dressed similarly and Sheila (his mother) drives by and notices that one of the young boys she just passed by has a similarity to her son Jack. So she pulls over, looks through her rear view mirror and realizes to her horror that it is indeed her son! She was so shocked that her very quiet, reserved son would dress so inappropriately. Yes, that could happen to anyone who isn't fortunate to be around your children often. They tend to just move with the crowd and could one day shock you out of your skin as was the case with Sheila.

Talk about spoilers, it is easy to say it only affects children of absentee , single or irresponsible parents. Consider the case of Bridget , a stay at home mother that left her job to be able to commit more time to her three young children and never noticed that one of her daughter's Tammy had tattoos on her chest. Not until an infection resulting from the unhygienic tattooing and piercing on her belly button brought this to her attention. Bridget was horrified to this discovery but more so was that all three of her children had tattoos on their bodies she had never seen! That must have been very hard to imagine that so much was going on that she had no idea of. Do you know what your kids are up to?

Let's take the case of a father of two called Drew. He had always wanted his Harry to be the best he could be. He created a relationship to harness good communication between them. Suddenly, he discovered that he hardly understood conversations when his son's friends came over to visit. These kind of revelations is what will jolt some of us to action as in the cases of Sheila and Bridget. As the saying goes "To be forewarned is to be for armed".

### Generation X

It still can be said that this generation is cultured if you take into account an aspect of the definition of the word "culture".

Culture can be defined as all the ways of life including, beliefs and institutions of a population that is passed down from generation to generation (oxford dictionary 2000). Culture has been called by many *"the way of life for an entire society"*. As such, it includes codes and norms of behavior such as law and morality, and systems of belief as well as the art. No mention if it was positive influence or negative.

"Generation X" as I would like to call the youngsters of today in my view can be said to be 'cultured' in their own way.

They have passed on arts, fads, beliefs, manners, games and dress codes that cut across borders, continents, race and religion. You just take a look around.

Pick out a typical teenager from Japan to Ghana (all other things being constant) and you would find this to be true. Unfortunately, the culture they pass down is a mixture of the good, the bad and the ugly.

Teens and young adults are very different today than they were decades, even centuries, ago. Now, subcultures of all sorts abound. Delinquent teenagers make it their goal to cause trouble for others. Gang culture is on the rise, with tattoos, hooded sweatshirts and knives as the norm. Authority figures are almost non-existent these days. Respect for others is severely lacking. Social skills are quite dysfunctional, bordering on non-functional in most societies today.

Let's start with what I classify as **THE BAD;**

## 1. *Slang*

Language, according to social scientists, is what differentiates humans from other animals. Language contains the symbolic meanings and shared consciousness of a society, whether it be the consciousness of class, ethnicity, geography or even age. Perhaps one of the most interesting facets of language is its mutability. Languages change from place to place, past to present, and among different age groups. One particular social phenomenon is the creation of social slang among various youth groups.

## The Common Denominator

Slang is generally a bit wittier and cleverer than Standard British English according to a study by Bethany Dumas and Jonathan Lighter. Slang is everywhere and youth slang, in particular, exerts enormous power.

Slang's primary reason for being, is to establish a sense of commonality among its speakers, which further ensures its widespread use. When slang is used, there is a subtext to the primary message. That subtext speaks to the speaker's and listeners' membership in the same "tribe." Because "tribe" identity is so important, slang as a powerful and graphic manifestation of that identity's benefits. At times, the primary message is not in the meaning of what is said, but in the very use of slang a compelling example of how the medium can be the message.

The four factors that are the most likely to produce slang are youth, oppression, sports and vice, which provide an impetus to coin and use slang for different sociolinguistic reasons. Of these four factors, youth is the most powerful stimulus for the creation and distribution of slang. For, although we are not all members of a group that is oppressed or sports fanatics immersed in the lore of the game, we were all young once. When you are young, you are subject to the generational imperative to invent a slang vocabulary that is perceived as your own, rejecting the slang of our older brothers and sisters (let alone our parents) in favour of a new lexicon.

Youth slang derives some of its power from its willingness to borrow from other bodies of slang. Despite its seeming mandate of creativity and originality, slang is blatantly predatory, borrowing without shame from possible sources.

Foremost among them is the African-American vernacular, whose influence on American youth slang of the 20th century cannot be over-stated.

Whatever its source, youth slang is a core element of youth culture, as a defiant gesture of resistance and an emblem of tribe or social identity.

Even the most vigilant and repressive attempts by adult authority cannot completely eradicate slang and music with its slang lyrics. Language can be scrutinized and controlled in some places at some times, but it defies universal regulation, which allows its subversive nature to prevail.

## 2. Graffiti

This is the name for images or lettering scratched, scrawled, painted or marked in any manner on property. Graffiti is sometimes regarded as a form of art and other times regarded as unsightly damage. It could also be termed as indiscriminate displays of signature mark. In most parts of the world the menace of graffiti is considered to be a criminal offense.

This street art is similar all over the world and though the languages of the art may differ, the perpetrators have a common goal, to send their defiant message to the society. It is usually an easy means to protest a vague sense of hurt or deprivation which sometimes is true but most often has become a "youth thing." Most graffiti art work shows the talent and ambience' of the artist and if properly harnessed and groomed could be the next great thing in the art world (if only they knew that). I once spoke with a known graffiti offender and asked why he didn't make a career out of his artistic skill instead of using it to get him in trouble and he looked at me and said,

*"If I make money off the graffiti, then am a looser. Money is not the point".*

However your views of graffiti, the menace has come to be a youthful protest culture, whose language from Jamaica to Netherlands is the same.

## 3. Loud music

This is another youth culture that expands all races and religions. Generally, loud music is an "in-thing" and most of us can remember our parents asking us to turn down the volume of the radio and jukeboxes as the case maybe. One often wonders when you're older why that was so and the answer simply would be it sounded better loud or so we thought.

Some young people say they enjoy loud music because then they can crank up the volume and listen to their favourite songs loud and clear. Also, so they can hear every beat and maybe so other people can hear it too. One common reason for people to turn up their music so loud is so that they can drown out all the surrounding sounds around themselves. Or maybe they could disappear from the world. Another reason is because it could be calming to that person and may take away and problems or stress they may have.

Today, its a greater menace to society because technology has evolved such that your music can be carried with you everywhere you go in forms of portable CD's to ipods and mp3 players. As such it could be heard on the street, on the bus, train and even in a public toilet!

Did you know that nearly half of young people experience hearing problems after being exposed to loud music.

According to research by the Royal Institute For Deaf

People (RNID).The increased exposure to loud music

threatens to create a generation who develop

hearing problems in middle age!

## 4. Gangs;

Being part of a gang doesn't necessarily mean you're more likely to use a weapon, but offending in a group could impact on the level of crime committed.

According to research, almost 1 in 10 teenagers are members of a gang. If you're in a gang, it's said you're more likely to:

- have friends who are in trouble with the police;
- have run away from home;
- have been expelled or suspended from school;
- Be drunk on a frequent basis.

### What makes a gang?

The term 'gang' is used in many different ways by the media, police, community organizations and the Government. Definitions range from 'a group of young people hanging around shopping centres' to 'organized criminal gangs'.

A report published by the British Home Office in

2004 defines a 'delinquent youth group' as:

- Young people who spend time in groups of three or more;
- A group who spends a lot of time in public places;
- A group that has existed for three months or more;
- A group that has engaged in criminal or delinquent behaviour in the last 12 months;
- A group that has a name, an area, a leader, or set of rules.

Of those belonging to a gang, 13% admitted to carrying a knife and 1% to carrying a gun. This compares to 4% of non-gang members carrying a knife and less than 1% a gun. However, a report by the Bridge House Trust, *'Fear and Fashion - The use of knives and other weapons by young people'*, claims there is no 'convincing' evidence to prove that belonging to a gang drives young people towards carrying knives or other weapons.

"There are two distinctly different types of gangs. First of all we've got a gang that's a collective group of individuals who wake up in the morning and do nothing but crime," says Michael Jervis,an officer at London Borough of Waltham Forest and part of the Defendin Da Hood initiative . "Then we've got a second tier we call 'crews', who although will use crime to feed their status level, don't necessarily have a focus of living a life of crime every day of the week.

"Unity in any spectrum is a good thing and there are positives and negatives that can be drawn from all types of unity. What is bad is when you get that connotation wrong and you start using it to affect the way you behave."

*Gang experience*

Luke, 19 years-old, used to live in a low income estate in Sheffield. "From my experience, a gang is a group of people who give themselves a name and go about life imposing their name and their rule upon others - often using violence.

" Luke recalls;

*"Truth is, living in a council estate is like being part of a community. Anyone who's lived in one will know that regardless of what you do - if you're a student or a worker, or you sit on your ass smoking weed all day - some people in the community will want to transform you into one of them. I don't mean they will rob you or mug you, but by being friendly and showing you respect, it leads you to think you have things in common with them. I started smoking weed like this. People from gangs learn early on in their lives the drug and violence world. Some are manipulated by it, and for many, it's the only future they know."*

Peer pressure and wanting to look 'bad' are two of the reasons people join gangs, but during my investigation, one thing seemed to stand out. Young people are searching for some kind of family unit.

Chris Saed is a youth worker at Sulgrave Youth Club, a place that gives young people something to do during the week nights and keeps them from falling into things like gangs. He had this to say about why more and more youth are joining gangs.

*"I think what gangs offers you in comparison to a family are security and protection. Being in a gang means you always have someone watching your back, and people that feel they don't have that protection and support at home will look elsewhere for it."*

Michael Lewis, another youth worker opined that;

*"There are many reasons to why young people get into gangs. The main reason is just to have friends. Peer pressure can lead people into a situation where there is a need to feel like you belong to something. It can seem like a family, not all families are good though, but some are. It depends on what your gang does. You could be in a gang that helps old people across the road. A youth club is a gang, but not a negative one."*

Once you're in a gang it can be hard to break free. But 22-year-old Kemar did.

*"When I was a kid, a gang was just being bad, troubling people, not to the full extent of stabbing someone but obviously harming them. Punching or kicking them; belittling them in front of people. We didn't have guns or knives. We were actually scared to use knives. It was only the few that used knives to make a big point, and this isn't going back too long ago. But we were scared most of the time. We weren't really troublemakers we were just doing it to fit in."*

I doubt gangs will fade away. People always want to fit in and even if it's in the bad or wrong crowd or the right crowd, people just want to fit in. Right? Would you know if your child belonged to a gang?

*THE UGLY*

*5. Body piercing;*

The word piercing can refer to practice of body piercing or to an opening in the body created by this act. The cultural norms reflected in body piercings are various. They may include religion, , fashion, eroticism, or sub cultural identification.

Body piercing has been a popular method of self-expression since ancient times. Roman centurions wore nipple rings to show their virility and courage, Amazonian warriors put heavy metal rings through their noses to intimidate their enemies, and ancient Egyptian royals had naval piercing to prove their high status in society.

Today, although still associated with tribal people such as the Masai warriors of East Africa, body piercing has become a popular fashion in western society. This has been made widespread in Britain by punk culture in the mid 1970s. Piercing the ears, nose, navel, tongue, and other parts of the body has now become commonplace, particularly among teenagers and young adults. One in five piercings now leads to infection (Department of Human Services, Victoria).

Emergency medical technicians recently wheeled a 19 year-old girl who had stopped breathing from a drug overdose into a Westchester City hospital. Doctors tried putting a breathing tube down her throat, but their path was blocked by three 1-inch-long metal stud barbells running along the length of her tongue.

One doctor got to the point where he said ;

*'If you have to rip her tongue, just do it."*

Eventually they got the tongue out of the way, but her body piercing could have cost her her life.


### *Things you need to know about piercings*

The popularity of piercing various body parts continues to increase, from mainstream thirty-some things to rebellious teenagers, and they are piercing their bodies in stranger and stranger places - in the mouth, on their navels, through cheeks and even in the genitals.

But doctors are starting to see more of body piercings disadvantages: oral piercings are causing swollen tongues, excessive bleeding, infection and swallowing of small jewellery parts. In fact, infections from moist or unclean piercing sites now occur in about one out of every five piercings (Ferguson Ward,1994).

Those receiving the piercings are firing back, however, saying that the majority of people know how to take care of themselves with disinfectants. But, according to some medical practitioners, many piercers are providing their services in unsafe environments - no gloves or mask, no sterilization equipment and usually very unsanitary surroundings.

Other hazards come later – when jewellery is removed from the piercing site. Skin dimpling may appear even though the hole has closed up. A second problem is celluloid's - where scar tissue extends into normal tissue. If a person receives a paper cut and develops celluloid, they may end up with a scar the thickness of a pen. Celluloid the size of a pea may develop on an earlobe where an earring once hung. Unfortunately, if you cut out celluloid, another may develop at the same location.

## *Caring For Those Little Holes*

Each body part presents its own specific danger, such as bleeding, nerve damage or infection and, therefore, requires special attention. Oral piercings, for instance, require an alcohol-free, anti-microbial mouth rinse. Alcohol isn't recommended because it increases the possibility of bleeding. Topical antibiotic creams should not be used for skin piercings because they prevent oxygen from reaching the wound to help it heal. In the upper part of the ear, a serious infection could cause the cartilage to die, leaving permanent disfigurement. Oozing pus from bellybutton piercings is also quite common.

Treating an infection can be difficult. For example, if someone receives an antibiotic to fight the "streptococcus" bacteria, it may be of no help because they actually need an antibiotic to fight the "gram negative" bacteria found in the mouth.

The most common piercing problem is ripped skin from the jewellery either catching on clothing or being pulled off. But maybe the most serious threat is hepatitis C. Hepatitis C is a blood borne infection that is being seen more and more in medical rooms, and doctors fear it may just be the tip of the iceberg. It causes cirrhosis and cancer of the liver and is the most common reason for liver transplants in the U.S. There is currently no vaccine for hepatitis C. Unsterilized equipment, poor follow-up care or the reuse of piercing needles all add to the risk of contracting hepatitis C. Only certain materials should be used in piercing, including titanium, surgical steel, 14-carat and 18-carat gold, and a plastic called Tygon or PTFE. Sterling silver should be avoided because it oxidises.

( Dr Micheal Vranken ,www.Kidshealth.com)

## 6. Drunkenness

This is a fast catching trend amongst our teenagers.

Of the many issues that jostle for priority in the new year, few have a greater claim for urgent attention by parents, police and politicians than the shocking increase in under-age drinking.

An investigation by "The Scotsman " in 2008 reveals examples of children as young as ten being arrested by the police for being drunk in public. Front line workers say the phenomenon is far worse now than a decade ago, with primary school pupils found in the street after drinking so much alcohol they are out of control.

In the past five years, ( according to ESPAD Report, 1994) more than 2,000 children have been arrested for being drunk and incapable in public. Of these, at least 34 percent were all aged 12years old or younger. These figures may fairly be said to be only the tip of the iceberg as far more cases will not reach the arrest stage, with youngsters instead being taken home or warned by law-enforcement officers. Over those five years, Scotland's biggest police force, Strathclyde, arrested 1,475 under-age drinkers, 30 of whom had not even reached their teens. The youngest was just ten. Rather than being taken home to their parents or educated about the risks they are taking, they are being trashed and arrested. The new figures, obtained using Freedom of Information legislation, show that in Grampian, 113 under-age drinkers were arrested, with the youngest only 12. Some of the most high-profile and tragic instances of child drinking have occurred in the area.Barely a year goes by in Scotland now without the launch – or tired re-launch – of drink-awareness campaigns designed to curb the huge personal and social cost of alcohol abuse. It is a blight on Scotland and one that the justice secretary, Kenny Mac Askill, has rightly taken to heart with measures designed to curb irresponsible selling of alcohol and in particular the sale of alcohol to under-age youngsters.

But a much broader assault is needed than measures targeted at licensees and shop managers. Binge drinking across all ages carries huge social, health, police and personal costs. It is a feature of modern life that needs to be tackled. But the phenomenon of pre-teenage drunkenness is particularly pernicious. It blights children and draws them into the criminal justice system – an indictment of the current levels of community cohesion, family and, above all, parental care.

Instances of children under the age of 12 being arrested in Britain's streets for drunkenness testify to a continuing failure of previous efforts and the need for a much broader and emphatic campaign, linking together programmes targeted at schools and parents as well as the liquor and drinks trade. Forceful and effective action is now imperative and the law should not shrink from impressing on parents the need to keep alcohol out of reach of children and, where necessary, to take action against parents who fail in this very basic responsibility. You might as well face the fact that at some point in their teenage years, your child will drink. It's part of growing up, becoming adult and testing boundaries they say. After all, most adults drink in Britain, the vast majority responsibly and in moderation.

But teenage drinking is a definite problem. Too many teens drink too much and too young - getting drunk has become part of a normal weekend for so many teenagers, whether in clubs or pubs, in parks or on the streets, at parties or at home.

What can parents do to stop the excessive drinking and teach teens to imbibe some sense of responsibility?

## By Example

If you don't drink in excess, there's a good chance your teen won't, either. Some say that the home is a good place to introduce teens to alcohol, and letting them experience the fact that a little, with a meal, can be pleasurable. More than that, it's a controlled environment where you can monitor and limit how much they drink. But you should also look at your own drinking habits: the more you drink, you more your teen is going to see that as acceptable and copy it.

It's probably best not to let them drink in the early teenage years. At that point their bodies haven't developed enough to really cope with alcohol. By the time they're around 16 they should be able to process it more easily.

## With Their Friends

Peer pressure can be an insidious thing. It often leads to excessive drinking, both among boys and girls. When your teen is out with friends there's little you can do to stop them getting drunk. But if you teach them about the dangers of alcohol, you can at least minimize the impact. Remind girls in particular that when drunk it's all too easy to end up having sex, for example. Also that no one should ever leave a drink unattended, whether in a pub, a club, or at a party. They don't know what someone's going to slip into it and what might happen after.

Alcohol can fuel aggressive behaviour. Emphasize that to your teens. Tell them it's okay to move to soft drinks if they begin to feel drunk, and not to mix drinks. You might not convince them to stay away from 'alcopops' or designer drinks, but strongly suggest they stick to one kind of alcoholic beverage all night. Remind them that they don't have to keep pace with the fastest drinker in the group.

If they're going out to a party or a club, make sure they eat a good meal first; it will help absorb the alcohol and reduce the possibility of drunkenness.

*Teens And Drunk Driving*

Teens feel they're indestructible, and often don't even realise they're drunk. An American idea that can help protect your teen from drunk driving is a contract between parents and children. They pledge never to drive drunk or get into a car with a friend who's been drinking. In return, you agree that they can call you at any time, even 4 a.m., and you will come and pick them up. It's not something to moan about when you're doing it. In fact it's promoting responsible behaviour and you should praise the teen for mature thinking.

Some teens will drink, and some of them will get drunk for the first time, and pay the price the next day. It's experience, and all you can do is help them learn from it and make sure nothing bad happens as a result.

## 7. Dress sense

Whatever happened to fashionable clothes-designer ranges etc.?Children these days can't be bothered about sensible modest dressing. It either has got to be torn, faded, painted or patched for it to be cool. The age these days has reduced to ten year old s! What are your children wearing?

Gothic, fetish or Elmo they call it could make you really jump out of your skin.

*Graciela's Story*

Graciela walked into a fast-food restaurant with her two young children and noticed a group of teen boys sitting at a table. They had spiked, brightly coloured hair and leather outfits with chains everywhere. "I bet their parents are ashamed of them," she thought.

She ordered meals, picked up the tray of food, and looked around for an empty table. The place was packed, and all the tables were full. She stood for a moment, with the loaded tray in her hands and her children clinging to her, when the group of teenagers dressed in punk attire suddenly stood up. A young man with green hair walked right up to her.

*"We're done, ma'am, please take our table,"* he said.

*"Let me carry that for you."*

He took her tray, walked to the table, and set it down carefully while one of his buddies took her children by the hand and led them to the table, and another teen brought over straws and napkins. She thanked them all for their help and kindness.

*"No problem,"* they answered and left.

She was shocked beyond words.

Her original thought was replaced by, "I'll bet those boys' parents are really proud of them."

Teenagers often wear clothes that adults can't stand. In our eyes, many teens' outfits make them look odd, clownish, grungy, too sexy, or downright scary. But the old adage, "Don't judge a book by its cover," is especially true with teens. A really nice, kind teen can be hiding underneath an unusual outfit. Your job as parent of a teenager is to find his/her inner qualities and focus on who she is, not what he/she wears.

Remember what you and your friends wore when you were teens? In the 1960s and 1970s long hair, tie-dye shirts, bell-bottom pants, and bulky hippie sandals drove parents crazy. Fashions and fads come and go, and your teen is bound to experiment with them. Show your teenager that you love and validate him/her even when his style differs completely from your tastes. Also let them know that people judge them principally by their looks.

If you still can't get past the outlandish outfits, try the following:

- *Look at other teens.* You may think that your teen dresses worse than anyone, but when you look at what others his/her age are wearing, you might start to think otherwise.

- *Enforce school rules.* Learn your teen's school dress code. If she tries to walk out the door wearing something that's against the code, remind her of the rules and ask her to change - and gently say that it wouldn't be fun for her to wind up in detention because of her outfit.

- *Consider your whole teen.* There's much more to your teenager than how she dresses. Is she happy? Is she doing well in school? Does she treat people with respect? Does he have healthy hobbies and interests? Is he staying out of trouble? If he's doing relatively well overall, then his outfit is a minor issue - perhaps even a non-issue.

- *Tell the truth.* If you see that what your teen wears might endanger him/her or cause her to miss opportunities, like getting that job she really wants, tell him/her. Just remember to do so calmly and in the most non-judgmental manner possible.

It's normal for a teen to express him/her through clothes. Step in if you feel that his attire is putting him at risk or is a sign of hidden problems, such as joining a gang or feeling poorly about himself. Talk with a school counsellor for guidance. Otherwise, accept her clothes, knowing that in a year or two her style will probably change again.

The 21$^{st}$ century spoiler list can go on and on. Let's make an effort to keep up and be alert to the possible changes, treats and dangers our youngsters face .

# Chapter Two

## What did you say?

*"That's Phat ,brotha innit?*

*"Checkout my ride" Said Chantee .*

*"Yea , all that and a bag of chips" replied Joel.*

For most people over the age of twenty-five, particularly bemused parents still struggling to understand the ever-shifting changes in teenage slang - this sentence will mean absolutely nothing. But for our teens it simply means;

*"That's cool isn't it?*

*"Check out my shoes.*

*"Whoa, that is very attractive."*

Today, communication with our teenage children can sometimes be a nightmare especially when they don't want you to be in on their conversations.

It has become such a problem that some big departmental stores like Tesco,(UK) came up with a guide book of slang's for their older workers to be able to relate better with their younger staff and customers.

Communication by definition is the process to impart information from a sender to a receiver with the use of a medium. Communication requires that all parties have an area of communicative commonality. This commonality is a wide gap between parents and their teens

So it's very important that in order to communicate properly you have to understand the language used.

Teens/young adults often speak a language of there own called slang. Understanding some of these slangs in practical terms help deal with issues arising from poor communication.

In my work with children, my first task was to learn the common slangs which helped me understand the children I worked with better. Honestly, I still can't understand why they like to speak this twisted, very complicated version of English but one thing I do know, it takes a lot to remember what each stands for.

I once asked a teenager I was mentoring why she spoke good English to me but when she was with her friends, she spoke slang and she simply told me she didn't want to be seen as stuck -up, not cool or old fashioned. Hmm! Leaves a lot to desire about being cool these days.

### *The Basics of Teenage Slang Conversation*

*"That couch is so gay. Excuse me?"*

*You're sick.*

*Actually, I feel just fine, thank you.*

*Oh! Man, jam dat hype!*

Does this sound like a teen in your life and the responses that automatically pop into your head while attempting to interact with them? While "gay" means stupid and "sick" is a positive thing, you may be completely overwhelmed by this new vocabulary sprouting out of your sweet child's mouth. If you can relate to this feeling of bewilderment and confusion, you are not alone.

In today's technologically savoury world, young people not only have typical teenage slang of their generation, but a whole slough of on-line jargon as well. However, let's put the latter aside for a moment and focus more on the basics of general conversation. Before you know it, you will be able to communicate with your offspring like you used to before that strange event called adolescence took over their lives. I will begin to explain a few of the most used slangs in detail.

### All That and a Bag of Chips

No, this doesn't mean that your teenager is ravenously hungry and looking for a good meal plus a bag of chips. In actuality, this is a youth's version of calling someone handsome or beautiful. Millennial coined this phrase to use when they are busy gushing about their crushes , idolizing movie stars, or just adoring a friend or mentor in general. Chances are when they use this phrase; they are talking about someone or something that they more than likely are not sharing their feelings about with you. Were you confused by its meaning? Then their plan worked.

### Butter

The food references tend to really run rampant on the teenage slang scene, and using the term "butter," again has no connotation with the cooking ingredient with which it shares a name. To say that something is butter means that is something really good. A popular L.A. nightclub has also recently stolen this lingo, capitalizing on the young slang that describes it as what we once referred to as trendy, hip, or out of this world.

### Flash

Is your child snapping back at you with a sound effect rather than the typical eye rolling? Well stiffen up that lip because they just called you stupid. "Flash!" is exclaimed by today's youth as a shortened version of "News Flash!" which in layman's terms means, "You just said something really obvious and stupid."

## Spun

A replacement for "cool," to say that something is "spun" means your teen really likes the way something looks. To say "Jamie's jeans today were spun," translates to he/she really liked the look of those pants. But, be careful not to strut around just saying the word spun like you would with cool....because that is certainly not cool, if you catch our drift. Spun needs to have other words to go with it, like the sentence example about the jeans mentioned previously. Saying"spun by itself will doom you towards a "Flash" .

## Tripping

If you hear a young person say "you're really tripping," don't panic. Gone are the days where "tripping" had an immediate drug attachment to it. While the word is still used to describe someone acting as if they are strung out on drugs, the term is used to describe anyone who is acting crazy, stupidly, or without good judgement. So hold back before you raid your teenager's room and search for evidence of a cocaine addiction. Chances are they have just borrowed this 1960s reference to describe their favourite friend with an out of the ordinary personality.

## Teen Slang's to Watch Out For;

While the words about definitely shouldn't send you tripping, there are in fact some versions of teen slang that parents should be aware of. Drug references have evolved along with the drugs of choice for today's teens. While previous generations may have feared getting caught smoking marijuana in their parents' house, today's teens are hitting raves including the hard narcotics more frequently and intensely than ever before. Here are some terms to watch out for, and to dig a little deeper if you overhear a cell phone conversation using them.

## Pilot

A co-pilot is a person's friend who has agreed to stay sober and hallucinogenic-free while another youth takes LSD or any other kind of narcotic. If you hear your teen talking about a co-pilot, either in reference to themselves or someone else, it is a red flag that he/she is hanging out in a crowd where drugs may be involved. "Ground man" is another term meaning something very similar.

## Guide

A guide is a dealer or experienced drug user who may be teaching your teen or another young person their first moves and steps into the drug world. A guide is the peer pressure instigator, the narcotics guru, and chances are the one that young people look up to when it comes to partying and getting high.

## Bagging

This term is used to describe the action of using inhalants in order to achieve a euphoric state. Inhalant drugs should be taken just as seriously as any others, and in some cases even more so. Protect your teen by asking questions and making more of an effort to meet their friends and cohorts if you hear a term such as "bagging" floating around the house.

## Bummer Trip

To hear that someone had a bummer trip is to suggest that they had a bad experience with a PCP. From an upset stomach to terrifying hallucinations, the sky's the limit with this damaging and destructive drug. Stay alert if you hear this slang in your teens life. Don't be afraid to be overprotective – it may be a choice toward life or death.

## Internet Jabber

With kids today chatting furiously into instant messenger windows and My Space pages loading all over the screen, a whole new evolution of teen slang has come about. Here is a handful of instant messenger lingo you may read by accident (or perhaps on purpose!) or that you may get in response to a message you send to a teen.

These are some of the common on-line teen slang:

AFK - *Away From Keyboard*

ASL - *Age/Sex/Location?*

BTW - *By The Way*

CTN - *Can't Talk Now*

JAS - *Just A Second*

IDC - *I Don't Care*

ILU - *I Love You*

JW - *Just Wondering*

LYLAS – *Love You Like A Sister*

NVM - *Never Mind*

POS/"9" – *Parent Over Shoulder*

SRY - *Sorry*

YTB - *You're The Best*

My favourite of these internet jabbers seem to be CTMOS which means "Can't talk, Mom over shoulders" Here are some more slangs to get you through with your teenage audience.

**A and B the C of D**: *Above and Beyond the Call of Duty*

**Am I bothered?**: *I don?t care*

**B in the D**: *Back in the Day*

**Bad**: *Good : this can also mean bad; when in doubt, just nod*

**Ballin**: *Doing well*

**Blood**: *Mate, chum*

**Brotha**: *Mate*

**Buggin**: *To act crazy or strange*

**Cane**: *To do something to excess*

**Cuss**: *Defame*

**Homeboy**: *A person who?s there for you like a brotha*

**How?s it hangin?**: *How are you today?*

**Innit?**: *Is n't? it? Is it? You know? Oh, really?*

**Is it blood?**: *You know, mate? Oh, really, mate?*

**Laters**: *Cheerio, goodbye*

**Minging**: *Ugly, unattractive*

**Nark**: *Annoy*

**Old skool**: *Old fashioned, dated, retro (can be derogatory or not)*

**Phat**: *Wicked, cool*

**Rank**: *Disgusting, horrible*

**Slammin?**: *Pleasing to the eye*

**Safe**: *That's OK*

**Safe blood**: *Brilliant, my brotha*

**Sound**: *That?s good, jolly good*

**Talk to the hand!**: *I'm not listening*

**Vexed**: *Stressed ,angry*

**Wack**: *Weak, boring*

**What you chatting? about?**: *Shut up, you're talking rubbish*

**Where it?s at**: *The coolest place to be*

**Word***: I understand, really*

**You get me?**: *Do you understand?*

**Biro:** *Bic / ball-point pen*

**Bob's your uncle**: *there you are*

**Flares:** *bell-bottoms*

**Pavement:** *pavement*

**Ring:** *call on the telephone*

**Skiving:** *to shirk away from doing any work*

**Snog**: *any kiss that isn't platonic*

**Sorry?:** *Huh? What?*

**Take the piss:** *to make fun of, to deflate one's Ego*

**Ta:** *Thanks (informal)*

**Mint/wicked**: *cool*

**Buff** : *fit*

**Dry:** boring

**Fo sho :** *yes*

**Fudge** : *a very stupid person*

**Howling :** *ugly*

**Cotch down** : *hangout*

**Chrips** : *chat up*

**Jack :** *to steal*

**Rago :** *whatever, ok*

**Rents :** *parents*

*Swag* : *scary*

**Unass** : *to leave or surrender*

*Yard* : *house*

*Rave* : *wild party*

*Beef* : *to fight, bully*

*Sick*: *to be cool*

Communication problems like these are numerous and varied. Some of the things that interfere with effective communication with your child, and some suggestions that will improve the quality of communication between you and your teenager, are discussed later. By using some of these concepts, it should become easier for you to talk with your child, and the resulting verbal interaction should increase in frequency and grow more meaningful.

### *Communication with Teens: Things to Remember*

1. Remember that during adolescence, communication generally decreases and a child will confide less in parents. This is a fairly normal process and should not be overreacted to.

2. Listen to what is being said; that is, try to understand the teenager's feelings and where he/she is coming from. Rather than thinking about arguments or retaliations, listen to him/her.

3. Stop what you are doing and look at the teenager. Listen when she speaks to you. Be sure that you are giving her the proper attention and that she is not talking to a newspaper or to your back.

4. Be sure most of your communication is positive, not negative. Don't dwell on mistakes, failures, misbehaviors, or something they forgot to do. Give them positive communication and talk about their successes, accomplishments, interests, and appropriate behaviour.

5. Talk to them about their interests (e.g., music, sports, computers, dance-team practice, cars, and motorcycles). Have conversations with them when you are not trying to make a point, to teach them something, or to impress them. Talk to them just to talk and to have positive verbal interaction.

6. Avoid talking too much - giving long or too-detailed explanations, repeating lectures, questioning excessively, or using other forms of communication that will result in the teenager turning a deaf ear to you.

7. Try to understand the teen's feelings. You do not have to agree or disagree with him; just make him aware that you understand how he feels. Do not try to explain away his emotions. There are times when you do not have to fix things or make the youngster feel better. Understanding how he feels may be the primary comfort that is needed.

8. Do not overreact to what is said. Remember, sometimes teenagers say things that are designed to get a reaction from their parents. In addition, do not say "no" too fast. Sometimes it is better to think about the request

and give a response later. In other words, think before you open your mouth.

9. Try to create situations in which communication can occur (driving the child to the doctor's appointment, having the teenager help you with household tasks). You have to be physically close to the teenager for communication to occur. A television in the adolescent's room can be an additional barrier to family communication. Whenever possible, the parent should try to do things *with* the teenager, rather than separately. Although the child may not frequently accept them, provide opportunities for him to do things with you.

10. Try to avoid power struggles, confrontation, and arguing matches. Your goal should be to have the communication move toward a compromise situation, rather than a battle. When appropriate, involve the teenager in decision making and setting consequences for his or her behaviour.

**The Information Drop Strategy:**

Every parent has some book or article that contains information that you would love your teenager to sit down and read. Usually it has something to do with hormones, puberty, and sexual behaviour. The big question is how to share these resources with your teenager in a way that captures his curiosity, or that at least doesn't nauseate him/her. In general, what worked so well when he was younger usually falls short during adolescence. Look back, years ago, if you made something important he accepted your evaluation and treated it as important, too. Now it's the opposite. If you want him to evaluate something as important, you need to undervalue it.

After raising a teenager of my own , I've come to realize that there are several ways to get them to read something that you think is important. One way is to leave the newspaper or magazine open to the article and leave it lying around carelessly on the coffee table or in the dining room. But by far and away the best option is to leave it in the bathroom. Yes! That's a sure fire read,just be judicious and save it for the really important stuff. Trust me on this one it works!

If ever there was sage advice from the front lines that was it. At the same time, there are other ways, too. Besides leaving it in the bathroom (which I agree is the best), it's also effective to leave the materials lying around in his/her room, preferably on her bed or desk. And after you leave the said book, do whatever it takes to not ask him/her if she saw it. Just trust that he/she found the book and will use it in a way that makes sense for her, which you probably won't find out about for at least a few months.

I was at the book store and found this great book on all the changes teenagers' bodies go through during and after puberty. I bought it and tossed it on my son's bed, but he never acknowledged seeing it. Given the state of his room, I couldn't even be sure that he had found it. One day I was fussing about the amount of rashes on his face and out of the blues  he goes-*"Its called puberty Mom. That book  you left in my room talked a bunch about how the hormone changes affect my skin, so I'm not too freaked out by this acne, since pretty much everyone gets it"*.

 I was shocked! Then he just went on to talk about the movie he was going to watch that evening, as if I had known all along that he had found the book and read it. Of course, when I stopped to consider that if he had read the parts about acne he had surely read the parts about sex and sexuality, I gave a huge sigh of relief.

The reality of these books is that they become references for your kids, something they turn to as various issues arise in their lives. Buy one book for your child to read if discussing the issues are difficult.

Here are a few actions you can practice to keep communication with your teen positive and ongoing:

*Use an upbeat tone of voice.* The intonation, volume and pitch of your voice can change the whole meaning of your words. Using an upbeat positive tone of voice will get you more attention than using a pessimistic tone of voice.

*Use eye contact when listening to your teen.* Eye contact shows the person who is speaking that you are interested in what she is saying and encourages more communication.

*Smile as much as possible.* Research shows that the face is the primary mode of communicating a person's feelings and the act of smiling can even boost a person's feelings. So when you smile, it will uplift your attitude toward what you and your teen are talking about, as well as your teen's outlook on what you are saying.

*Use open gestures.* Avoid finger pointing, crossing your arms and putting your hands on your hips. More positive movements like leaning forward and nodding will encourage your teen to share more about what she is thinking.

*Don't be afraid to touch your teen- keep the bond.* Hugs and goodnight kisses are still important, although your teen may wish to be asked first. Hold her hand when she needs to be consoled or give her a pat on the back when you are praising her. These touches convey our unconditional love for our children and should not be stopped just because your teen has gotten older.

*Watch Your Body Language*

When talking with your teen, it is important that your non-verbal communication cues support what you are saying verbally and not get misconstrued with how frustrated you are at work, for example. No one wants to talk to a grouch or someone who isn't really paying attention, which is what your non-verbal cues could be saying to your teen. Non-verbal communication, is often even more powerful than spoken words. Check your posture, facial expressions and gestures for the message they give. Are you focused on the conversation at hand or are you distracted? Be sure to give your teen your full attention, or they will feel that their issue is unimportant to you. Make eye contact and use cues like nodding to keep the conversation moving along.

### *Be Patient*

Kids may not be ready to spill their guts the first time you sit down to talk. Let them go at their own pace, and don't press them on issues they might not be ready to discuss. They are more likely to open up if they have the freedom to share when they are ready.

### *Communicating using a "problem-solving" model.*

There are six basic steps to any decision making model, though you can certainly tweak the steps to fit a particular circumstance or population. Some simpler problems may allow you to streamline the process, while more complex issues can benefit from the structure that this model provides.

- *Define the problem and set a goal for change.* This is the opportunity to verbalize what you would like to see happen. Try to be as clear as possible. The best goals are specific and measurable: For example, "Raise my Math grade to an 80" is much more helpful than "Do better in Math." Write it down so you have a constant reminder of what you are working towards.

- *Brainstorming options.* Come up with as many different ideas for attacking the problem as you can. This is the time to think outside the box. Don't stop to evaluate or criticize suggestions: the purpose of this step is to generate a free flowing exchange of suggestions. Ideas for the above goal might include things like: Get extra help from the teacher. Get a math tutor. Increase studying time. Get a study partner. Ask for study guides. Put all of the choices down on paper. Kids love this model.

- *Evaluate options.* Go back over each suggestion and take a second look. Is this idea feasible? What would I need to do to make this happen? Are their constraints (time, resources, etc.) that limit the possibility of this working? For example, the family budget might not allow for a tutor, but what about a study partner? Are their ways to broaden, tweak, or combine good suggestions to make them better?

- *Making a plan of action.* Choose the options you think will work best and formulate an action plan. Include the specific steps you will take for each choice. For example, if one piece of the action plan is "Increase studying to one hour a night," making a targeted plan about when, where, and how you will study might be helpful. Include a timeline with your action plan so you know when its time to evaluate how things are going.

- *Evaluation and Modification.* Assess how things are going. Is there steady progress towards your goal? Do changes need to be made in the plan? This is the time to revise the plan, if necessary. Cut out things that aren't helping, and possibly revisit the list made in the brainstorming step to see if you want to add anything new. Continue to evaluate and modify until the goal is reached.

### *Testing, Learning, and Attempted Independence*

What happened to your sweet young child? You know, the one who used to live in your house and greet you cheerfully, happy to see you and anxious to spend time with you. Be rest assured that child still exists, but he or she has become trapped inside the body of a teenager. The teen years are a time when children undergo great changes and transitions; they may want you to think you're not needed any more, but the reality is you're needed more than ever. One of the best ways to maintain connection and communication with your teen is to pay attention to body language and non-verbal cues they make.

Teenagers are testing their wings, so to speak, learning what it means to move from childhood to adulthood. That transition is not always smooth; it can be confusing, scary, and often proceeds in a 'two steps forward, one step backward' pattern.

It is the very nature of teenagers, though, to be reluctant to share what they're really feeling and thinking inside. They may feel silly, or not want to admit to their parents that they aren't as mature and independent as they would like to be. Despite this reluctance to open up and share, their true thoughts and feelings often still show through in their body language. You just have to know what you're looking for and pay attention.

### *Common Body Language of Teenagers*

Teenagers generally show most of the same body language as adults, but sometimes the non-verbal cues are more subtle or slightly skewed. Let's look at some common examples of teenage body language and what they generally mean:

***Slumped body posture*** – A teen that walks with slumped body posture may be feeling self-conscious, unhappy, stressed, or just a bit down. He or she might also feel pretty good, but is just lost in thought about something else .I was certainly guilty of this myself but I have come to learn shouting doesn't work.

***Poor eye contact*** – Teens often struggle to make eye contact, especially with adults. They haven't yet developed the self-confidence or comfort level of a full blown adult and so sometimes, they just can't quite look you in the eye. Go for a bike ride,take a drive in the car, just about any kind of activity where you are close enough to talk but not facing the added pressure of talking face to face. They would gradually build self confidence and trust.

***Just hanging around*** – Teens may have a tough time initiating conversation with their parents, so they sort of hang around in the background. They don't quite engage you directly, but they also don't head off and do something else on their own.

### Dealing With Body Language of Teenagers

So how, exactly, should you deal with this teenage body language? What is the best way to respond so that you and your teen keep connected with each other?

***Slumped body posture*** – The underlying meaning of this posture depends a great deal on what is normal for your teen. If it is his or her common posture, stay engaged and in touch but don't hover. Don't tell your teen to 'sit up straight' or anything like that, but do make yourself available for casual conversation. I was certainly guilty about this but Ive learned it does not work.

***Poor eye contact*** – If your teen has difficulty making eye contact with you, try to create situations where you can stay connected without having to look each other in the eye. Go for a bike ride, take a drive in the car, just about any kind of activity where you are close enough to talk but not facing the added pressure of talking face to face. Let them build trust gradually.

*Just hanging around* – If your teen is just hanging around, try engaging him or her in whatever activity you're doing. This non-verbal behaviour is quite often a sign your teen wants to spend some time with you, but is reluctant to come right out and say it. Take the lead yourself and find something to do together; your teen will probably be grateful for your effort. It could be watching a favourite tv programme, sport or even doing homework together.

**Take More Assertive Action**

Most parents struggle with knowing what action to take based on their teen's body language. Should they be worried? Should they be reassured? Chances are your teen will point you in the right direction, but you have to know your child's personality.

The time to take action and make yourself more assertively into your teen's life is when you see changes that are out of the ordinary for your child. A daughter who is normally talkative and perky but becomes quiet, reserved, and slumped over may have a problem that needs your attention. A son who is normally active and involved with his friends but suddenly hangs out with an entirely new group of friends or stops doing the things he used to enjoy may also have some underlying issue you need to address. Do not brush it aside or wish it away as some of us parents do. Try and find out what the problem is before it gets bigger.

**Real life stories**

Liz Thomson left home three years ago, fed up with the endless rows with her folks which began when she was 13. At 15, she was given much less freedom than most of her friends.

"At the time it seemed like my parents were really cruel. My friends' parents were very different. Mine were much too strict. They expected me not to go out at all. They controlled the way I dressed, because they always came with me when I went to buy clothes. We had a lot of arguments and differences of opinion"

Liz's parents were difficult in the way that parents have been difficult for generations. At the other extreme is a new breed of parents who unwittingly create problems by trying too hard to understanding.

Sebastian Finley is the envy of his friends. His mother is sympathetic and understanding. But in Sebastian's eyes, that's where some of his problems start.

"I know I've got a really nice mum. In a sense, she's the image of the perfect mother. But she's too understanding, she's too kind. On the surface we seem to have a great relationship, but really there's a distance. I can't tell her things because I feel she would understand too much. It's very important for me to have things that she doesn't understand. I need to be recognized as a teen and I need to be misunderstood sometimes."

Hugh Jenkins, director of the Institute for Family Therapy, says there are problems with both extremes: 'With parents who are totally liberal, completely accepting, it's a question of what does the child have to do to be taken notice of ? How extreme does it have to be? If a parent is always saying 'Yes, dear', where are the limits? At the other extreme, with a parent who is constantly screwing down the sanctions, the child either buckles under or fights fire with fire.'Which are you ? Learn to strike a balance.

# Chapter Three

## Who are you?

Remember the crazy fads in the late 70's and 80's? The tie-dyed shirts, the beads,shoulder pads, headbands, and the peace symbols? When I was in high school my dad hated my brothers bushy sideburns and afro hair, and my purple bell bottoms and colourful headbands. It was a fad to look like the rock idols of the day and that look was in. My appearance made no sense to my parents, but it made a lot of sense to me at the time.

I bet there are things your parents didn't like about the way you dressed as a teenager. Chances are, you don't still dress that way, and when you look at those old pictures you may giggle, as I do, about how silly you looked back then.

Today, I mostly hear from concerned parents of teenage girls who want to dress too seductively. They wonder how to deal with the issue of seduction when it has become so pervasive in our culture.

Teens today live in a world of sexual innuendo, where outward packaging and presentation is all important. The definition of modesty has changed for them, not so much because of the lack of values taught by parents, but because of the overwhelming exposure given to seductive lifestyles, that is what we should check as parents.

For the most part, girls dressing seductively is just a fad, and all fads pass soon enough. If your teen wants to be in on the fad of the moment, it doesn't mean much of anything about her character, other than that she is playing out a role on the stage of adolescence. Generally speaking, she hasn't gone off the deep end just because she wants to wear current fashions.

*KEY POINT*: Make sure he/she understands that modesty is an important part of your family's values and that's not an area you'll allow to be compromised, no matter what the current culture or fad says and put your foot down on it!

Teenage fads can be a challenge for most parents to manage. Since the internet, coupled with books, television, music videos and movies, have all inundated our kids with seductive images and inappropriate suggestions. Highly sexualized lifestyles are touted as normal, so girls face extreme social pressure to look and act seductively as well.

Some girls from good Christian homes often tell me they are torn between doing what is acceptable by their peer group to "fit in," and doing what is taught them by their families and church. More times than not, the social pressures for the teen to look and act like their peers will win out when they are in school or out with their friends. But they soon more often than not realize that the end result of their seductive presentations when the guys that do pay attention are not always what they expected, or what they really wanted in the first place.

My advice for parents is not to flip out when your daughter is just trying to fit in. Using harsh words that defame her character such as, "you look like a ..." will only push her deeper into the negative behaviour. Rather, calmly and regularly address the more important issue of modesty. Focusing on modesty, versus putting down the current fashion as our own parents did with us, will eliminate the perceived generation gap. And that way, when the next fad comes along she'll understand her boundaries within that fad as well.

Teenagers are infamous for being on the cutting edge of current fads and trends. The reason why teens are on the lookout for something new and different is almost a given: they are working on their identity. Your teen wants to identify with something that makes him/her feel good about him/her self. Something new comes out, all the teens and their peers check it out. If it sticks for a little while, it's a fad. If it sticks around for a longer time, it becomes a trend.

Many fads are harmless. Back in my day people cut the sleeves and collars of sweatshirts off and wore them inside-out. No big deal. This fad did not become a trend and is no longer seen. Today, everyone owns an Ipod and will text friends on their cell phones. These fads will either fade with new technology or become a trend and stay around awhile. We'll have to wait and see.

Some teen fads are dangerous. Huffing is one dangerous fad that comes to mind. Some kids can get pulled into a dangerous behaviour, such as drug use, because something like huffing is the current fad. It is a another good reason for parents to be conscientious of the warning signs of drug use .

While keeping up with teen fads can sometimes be exhausting for parents – especially for parents of pre teens who are just getting started – it is a worthwhile endeavour. Just because you can't pick and choose which fads or trends your teen will pick up, doesn't mean you don't get to add your opinion and use the fad as a teachable moment. Here's a few tips on how to keep up with your teens fads:

- Talk to your teen about the current things he/she is doing.

- Pay attention to the media your teen is using. Read his/her magazines, check-out his/her social networking page and watch his/her television shows. You don't have to know everything, but knowing what your teen is talking about when talking to you about the current 'in' things will help your communication with him/her.

- If a fad doesn't go against your morals or family values, allow it. You don't have to be a permissive parent to pick and choose your battles and not to sabotage your teens social life.

- Get your teen involved in something he/she enjoys –art, dance, sports, karate, etc. can influence some fads he/she may pick up.

- Sit back and enjoy it. Take pictures and save the memories. The best part will be sharing those with your grandchildren.

While it is true that teens start spending more time with their friends and are influenced by these peers through peer pressure, parents need to remember one simple truth: your teen will never forget the values you have given him. He may not always remember to use this better judgment and peer pressure may be the reason he forgets, but these values will make it through the trials of adolescence and into his young adulthood. Our job as parents is to give them the tools needed to use.

## *TEEN FASHIONS*

She sat across from me in the train, legs crossed and a picture of confused beauty on her face. I usually would not stare but she really captivated me. She had six rings on her ears, pierced tongue and lips , black lipstick with matching black lined smoked eyes, her dress was simple but black. Three red metallic studded belts hanging loosely off her hips. To compliment this very interesting garbs she wore,a long silver necklace with a pendant of a skull on it, black netted tights,and a pair of knee high platform boots from the sixties. And yes, her hair had strands of blue weaved in.

Still wondering why I stared at her?A few months later, I discovered that the dress code I saw is called Emo.

### 1. Emo Fashion

What is Emo?

The term "Emo" originally stemmed from a genre of punk music in Washington, D.C. These days, Emo refers to a fashion trend rather than music. Emo fashion styles today do not seem all that distant from Goth styles.

The latest trend is Emo (emotional) style as my son rightly corrects me. Emo style is definitely for those who adore bright colours. Green, pink, red, yellow matched with black will undoubtedly make you noticeable. If you are into this style, you must have an appropriate hairdo: Zelda hairdo for girls and jet black mop top for boys with Mohawk hairstyle. Pencil or at least cigarette-shaped jeans with studded belt is also a must-have. Rules for top are not that strict, you may choose anything you want, just be sure it's close-fitting and bright coloured. You must wear large amounts of jewelry and it's even better if you pierce your face (small lip ring would do perfectly). Emo style is perfect for those who wear glasses - it's a great accent and Emos love nerdy ones.

Believe it or not , most Emo kids are well behaved straight -A , high achieving students who feel being Emo is the only way to fit in.


A new Russian law could make being an Emo  illegal in the eastern European country (NMNews,2009).

Legislation is currently being formulated in Russia to heavily regulate Emo websites and ban Emo and goth dress styles in schools and government buildings. The new laws are apparently being driven by fears that these "dangerous teen trends" encourage depression and suicide. The legislation was presented this year at a hearing held by the State Durma, where critics claimed that the "negative" Emo culture encourages anti-social behaviour and glorifies suicide. Emo kids were described as teenagers who wear black, have facial piercings and black hair with fringes that "cover half the face", reports The Guardian.

The weekend saw mass protests by Russian Emo kids. In Krasnoyarsk, Siberia, where laws are already being implemented, protestors in a march held signs saying "A Totalitarian State Encourages Stupidity". Dmitry Gilevich of Russian emo band MAIO stepped in backing the protests, saying: "Expressing psychological emotions is not forbidden in Russia by law.

What is your take on all of this as a parent.I bet your're probably wondering is that what they call it?

### Shirts

Emo T-Shirts for both boys and girls are tight , typically T-shirts depicting skulls, cute drawings or band names. These band names should be Emo or indie bands. If it's cold out, some Emo teens wear tight long-sleeved T-shirts under their other short-sleeved shirts. They sometimes call it double vest or layering.

### Jeans and Skirts

Cute Emo skirt when it comes to jeans, once again boys and girls prefer them tight. The jeans are also low-rise and long enough to cover the tops of shoes. Some girls will wear skirts, as well, and these are usually flutter skirts, very short and almost ragged or skirts with a scarf-style appearance. Also, checked Scottish -style skirts are worn with a big safety pin at the side.

### Hoodies

Emo teens prefer to layer their clothes rather than wear jackets. So if the weather doesn't permit just a T-shirt, emo teens will wear hoodies over their layers of T-shirts. Some will even layer hoodies over lighter hoodies.

Shoes are simple looking and fairly practical. Most will wear converse, vans or converse-style shoes and high-heel boots. All shoes are platforms or canvas, perfect for drawing on.

## Accessories

Accessories are a must. Some typical accessories are belts, wide bracelets or arm bands, and large sunglasses. In cold weather, some emo teenagers will wear layers of scarves and fingerless gloves. Most girls do not carry a purse but use messenger bags instead. Of course, messenger bags with indie-band logos on them are preferred over plain. If a girl is wearing a skirt it is most often patterned and short.

## 2. Sagging

*Sagging* is a manner of wearing pants or shorts below the waist, revealing some or all of their underwear. This is usually worn by boys.

## Origin of Sagging

Sagging is commonly attributed in the media to have originated in the prohibition of belts for prisoners as belts could be used to commit suicide by hanging oneself, or to strangle others, or to use as a weapon in fights. In the early 1990s, hip-hop artists popularized the style.

Controversy of saggin in the United States of America;

In June 2007, the Town Council of Delcambre, Louisiana passed an indecent exposure ordinance, prohibiting people wearing trousers which show their underwear.

In March 2008, the Hahira, Georgia City Council passed a controversial clothing ordinance, in the name of public safety, that actually bans citizens from wearing pants that are below the waist and reveal skin or undergarments. The council was split 2–2, but the tie was broken by the mayor.

Benetta Standly, statewide organizer for the of Georgia stated;

*"In Atlanta, we see this as racial profiling... It's going to target African-American male youths. There's a fear with people associating the way you dress with crimes being committed."*

Sagging is very common amongst Blacks and the style of clothing is a violation of some school dress codes.

The interim police chief of Flint, Michigan ordered the arrest of saggers for disorderly conduct, though, as of July 2008, only warnings had been issued. The local chapter of the ACLU, saying that sagging does not violate the Flint disorderly conduct ordinance, has threatened legal action in response. Let your children know the history of saggin the ask them if they honestly want to be profiled as criminals. I've used this subtle method to convince some children to "Pull-up their pants" and to my surprise it works!

There was a time when having your underwear exposed might have caused great embarrassment. Today people show their underwear on purpose and with pride because it's deemed fashionable. And it's called saggin', wearing pants below the waist so that underwear is in full view. Sagging is not only for boys. Girls have caught on too and also have their own style of sagging called the" T-cut"( which is wearing a g-string pant that shows above a low-cut trouser).

The fashion actually transitioned from prison culture, said author-youth advocate Judge Greg Mathis of the "Judge Mathis" show.

*"In prison you aren't allowed to wear belts to prevent self-hanging or the hanging of others,"* said Mathias,Who at 17 once served eight months in jail.

*"They take the belt and sometimes your pants hang down. The same with no shoestrings in your shoes. You aren't allowed to have shoestrings. Many cultures of the prison have overflowed into the community unfortunately."*

Saggin' also has sexual connotations in prison.

*"Those who pulled their pants down the lowest and showed their behind a little more raw, that was an invitation," said Mathis. "[The youth] don't know this part about it. I always tease and tell them that they better be careful because some man who has been in prison 30 years who comes home and doesn't know any different may think it's an open invitation."*

Pastor Dianne Robinson of Jacksonville, Florida, is a crusader against the saggin' look.

*"I think it is a very disrespectful act," she said. "Sometimes they have on two and three pairs of underwear and most of the time it's not clean."*

The 64-year-old Robinson, founder of the Nanas and Papas Raising Grands Organization, has launched a campaign to end saggin'. She has started a belt collection for young men called "Pull Up Your Pants--Need Some Help, Here's A Belt!" On June 4, she plans to collect belts at the Ribault Family Resource Center at Ribault High School in Jacksonville.

*"It has gotten out of hand. People want to say something, but I think they are complacent," she said. "It's like a fad, but they don't understand where it came from. It was easy access in prison and it let the rest of the population know they were taken. It came from being connected to someone. A lot of guys don't know this. Every time I see a young man with saggin' pants, I wonder, 'What are you up to? What are you really up to?'"*

Robinson isn't the only one fighting the fashion. Last year a Dallas school trustee recommended a ban of the fashion at a City Council meeting. In 2004 a Louisiana lawmaker proposed House Bill 1626, also known as the Baggy Pants Bill.It would have fined offenders up to $175 or given community service. The Virginia Senate considered imposing a $50 fine on people who reveal their underwear to the masses. None of the bills passed. A Florida senator is currently trying to sponsor legislation to ban saggin' at public schools.

Mathis said the style is part of a destructive subculture.

*"Young people have given up on society as a result of the obstacles they face. Instead of fighting back, they join the subculture of drugs and crime as a means of what they believe will uplift them from poverty. So you have this inner change of what is cool and hip in the 'hood and what is cool and hip in prison. You have a rotating door."*

He added, *"I want to challenge our Brothers to pull up their pants and lift up their head ... We're no longer slaves. We are free to fight back, and that's what we must do."*

*"Saggin-rules!"* Said Bennard.

Not everyone agree to this.

*"Saggin is the coolest fashon statement ever! I'm white and where I live all the cool white kids sag their pants. It is sweet. Think about it -- your parents probably didn't like the current fashion's at the time, but ya gotta just get used to it. Go saggers and keep on saggin"* said Mickey

*"Saggin' is just a fashion trend. It is terrible that there would be a law against it. There is a lot of people in the world that think females expose*

*themselves to much. Maybe we should fine every female that show their bra strap. There should not be a law on an opinion"* said Chelle.

What is your opinion on saggin?Mine is simple."keep your pants up". Remember, what you believe is what you will enforce.

### 3. Tattoos/piercing:

You may have taken your daughter to get her ears pierced when she was in elementary school, so now you're shocked that she wants extra holes not just on her ears but on her tongue and eyelids as well. Or worse still , your son wants them too!Go figure.(You ought to be smarter than that).

Tattoos and body piercing (nose rings, nipple jewelery and belly button rings) are some of the latest forms of self expressions amongst modern day teens.

Like another serious discussion, you would like to have with your child , its important to find out all you can about the issue in order to have a smooth sell.

Body piercing, if done properly under hygienic conditions is really  not harmful! (Surprised?) Unfortunately,the profession isunregulated in most areas and many consumers are getting pierced under unsafe conditions( at school toilets, a sloppy tent at a music festival,or a corner shop at the local mall).

A key seller for discouraging tattooing and body piercing is the health risk. The idea of contracting an infectious disease most often works .The risk is the same as anyone that shares needles- from Hepatitis B/C to AIDS!

My favourite reaction to a tattoo when an acquaintance saw a friend's tattoo of a dog on his arm. She took one look and said "aren't you afraid of how it will look when you are older and the skin starts to sag!"   Kind of stuck with me.  I don't have a tattoo. I'd probably not be happy if one of my kids got one before they were old enough to make sound decision (like when they are about 50). But I'll cross that bridge when I get there I guess!

*To tattoo or not to tattoo?That is a very common question these days that put most parents in a dilemma of sorts.*

A dad named Maurice wrote us with a real hot question. His teenage son is active in the church and well respected by almost everyone ... and he wants to get a tattoo.

We'll dive in and address this, but I'm not going to tell you what to do, because every father and every family is different. The key question is this: Whose decision is this your child's, or yours? And my answer is, It depends on your approach to parenting.

On one hand, I can support the father who tells his teenager, "Tattoos are not an option while you're living in our house." Of course, that father should be ready to give his reasons, and he'd be wise to set that rule in place before the issue comes up.

Ten years from now, your son may regret having a tattoo on his arm or his chest, but on the other hand, you both may regret the fact that you have a distant relationship because of the blow-up you had over a tattoo.

No matter what you decide, I want to provide some ideas for you to think about. Because whether you're explaining your decision or advising your child about his or her decision, you need to be ready to talk about this issue—and the larger principles involved.

Now, we know it's hard for teenagers to imagine they'll ever be our age someday - with different tastes and different priorities. But you were a teenager once and it might be instructive and humorous to pull out old photos of yourself with an outdated hairstyle ,mutton chop sideburns ,and show them to your teen. Point out that the bad fashion decisions you made were temporary and you're glad about that. But, tattoos are pretty much forever.

Taking another approach, you might tell your teen that even though you know what great kids they are, and you don't judge them by their looks, other people (and maybe some relatives) might make certain assumptions based on the fact that they have a tattoo. What if a girl he wants to date or an employer he wants to work for doesn't like tattoos? Your child should know that some employers and even some summer camps have a policy of no visible tattoos. Help him see down the road a few years, and hope he takes all this into account.

Or just talk about the reason for the tattoo. Is it to feel accepted? Is it some kind of rebellion? Is she trying to stand out from the crowd? She may not identify her reasons in those terms, but you may uncover some deeper issues that need to be addressed. And, it could be that identifying the deeper reason and talking about that will take some of the "fun" out of getting the tattoo.

I know it's a tough issue. But however you handle it, strive to be understanding and avoid jeopardizing the future of your relationship with your teenager.


### *Are your teens piercing a statement?*

Some teens choose piercing as a statement of rebellion against parental values, while others are merely exhibiting a personal preference.

Joy Reeves' daughter Regina took calculus during junior year at her Midwestern high school and got an "A" the first semester.

*"Wow!"* Joy told her.

*"I ought to buy you a car."*

*"Actually, Mom,"* Regina replied,

*"I'd rather have my navel pierced."*

Joy was stunned.

*"I can't really say I was against it,"* she recalls,

*"Except that I never personally felt the need to buck the system as strongly as Regina does when I was young."*

Joy did allow the navel piercing. Now, four years later, Regina attends Mills College in Oakland and still wears her navel ring. She assures her mom that she is the most normal-looking girl in her college dorm room.

### *On the Rise- be alert!*

More and more parents are finding themselves faced with similar dilemmas. Based on nationwide anecdotal evidence, body piercing eyebrows, nose, tongue, chin, navel, and genitals is on the rise among teenagers.

Piercing is not new.

*"There have been people doing these piercings for hundreds or thousands of years,"* says John,

who self-pierced his genitalia more than a decade ago, and prefers to not use his last name. "Certain tribes in Africa and North America were doing piercing long ago, as well as European sailors and carnival performers."

Today, however it is teens and young adults drawn to the piercing frenzy in droves. In some cases they are all dangerously piercing themselves in order to wear the shiny body adornments so craved by their generation.

At age 24, John, who now lives in Colorado, self-pierced his genitals in what is referred to as an Ampallang piercing (horizontally through the head of the male genital) penis). By his own admission, he says the piercing was risky and he was foolish to do it himself.

*"My piercing bled a lot, and I fainted not long after I did it,"* he says.

Luckily he had two friends with him who helped to revive him.

*"It's hard to say why I did this,"* says John.

*"I guess it was a kind of rite of passage for myself."*

He had heard that the piercing would intensify sexual pleasure for both partners, but acknowledges that he and his girlfriend at the time didn't notice much difference.

Self-piercing, unfortunately, is more prevalent today than ever. Although it carries with it risks of self-mutilation, infection, and serious complications, teens often have a cavalier attitude toward piercing their own body parts.

*"It's a developmental issue. They think they are invulnerable,"* says Lynn E. Ponton,M.D, a child and adolescent psychiatrist.

*"They take risks because they think, 'Nothing bad can happen to me.'"*

A professor at UC San Francisco, Ponton is the author of "**The Romance of Risk**": Why Teenagers Do the Things They Do (Basic Books, 1997).

A sense of thrill or risk-taking can make self-piercing seem like an acceptable adventure, similar to the thrills of bungee jumping or drag racing in teens of previous generations. It may also seem like the only alternative to teens whose parents won't give permission for a piercing. Show them that there are better alternatives and the dangers of bad piercings and tattoos.

# Chapter Four

## What do you think?

Ethics is defined (wikipedia) as a body of moral principles or values governing a particular culture or group of people. It is generally doing the right thing when no one is looking.

School/workplace ethics are governed based upon the personal ethics of those who are I authority .Your ethics are usually an extension of the personal standards or lack of them that is inherent in the people who make up the workplace. To a large extent, we are shaped by our cultural settings and its values imprint themselves on our minds in ways most of us hardly notice.

Since ethics deal with the formation and expression of character, there is no better place to begin their development than in the family home.

Here is a list of ethics children need to learn to give them a head start in school or at their places of work later in life.

- Treat others with dignity and respect.
- Respect those in authority over you.
- Handle all transactions with honesty
- Keep to time for every occasion and activity.
- Treat the property, equipment and belongings of others with care.

*What are some practical workplace behaviour ethics?*

Phil Drake was three days old in his new job as a project assistant at a high end management firm. Shaun was his line supervisor and and project manager assigned to guide him through the first week.

Shaun and Phil were working on a building project at work for the past four hours. Shaun went over to his desk across the large office to get a file to refer to some similar work he did last year only to get back and Phil was gone. Suddenly, the telephone rang in the office they both shared. It was a call from Phil's wife so Shaun asked her to call back in ten minutes convinced that Phil had probably just dashed off to the bathroom in a hurry.

After a while, Phil did not show up so Shaun decided to go look him up for it seemed odd that he would spend so much time in the toilet. To his surprise, Phil was not there. Shaun then decided to ask around in case he got lost in the building as it was Phils first week at work and was still trying to get use to the daunting office block when Carol the receptionist said she saw him leave the building a few minutes ago, guessing he was off for his lunch.

Thirty minutes later, Phil saunters into the office and to Shaun's amazement discovers by Phils own admission that he had gone off for lunch! Shaun was stunned that he did not have the courtesy to let him know of his decision in the middle of a meeting.

Phil's story is a result of throwing ethics and common sense decency to the wind .Such indiscretions could cause us friendships, jobs, contacts and even pain. But this is an all too familiar case in most workplaces as little courtesies are no longer accorded to colleagues. Where did it all go wrong? Your guess is as good as mine- at home!If Phil was your child, would you be proud of his behaviour?

Practical workplace behaviour ethics are a matter of remembering that things should be done "decently and in order" . In other words, there needs to be a basis for ethics that stems from something deeper than the immediate situation or human viewpoint. One can rationalize any choice or decision they make. However, these methods fail to give someone a clear moral compass. Therefore, one's personal behaviour in the workplace has to be based on a solid ethical foundation .

The word "decently," in the passage cited above, comes from a Greek root word that means honestly or in a seemly manner. In a world where honesty is not highly prized and situational ethics abound, having a reputation for honesty in business dealings will not only bring peace of mind but will also reap reward. That means that one's workplace behaviour ethics of honest treatment for all: employer, fellow employees, vendors, and customers is a hallmark to be prized and not despised. It would be great if these ethics began at the top of the company. However, whether that is true or not, the call for decent and orderly behaviour in the workplace should be the minimum standard by which every individual in the company operates. This means we understand that situational ethics do not result in personal integrity. Show good example,then trust that your kids will follow you.

The word "order" in this same passage means an arranging, arrangement, a fixed succession observing a fixed time, due or right order, orderly condition, the post, rank, or position which one holds in civic or other affairs. Since this position generally depends on one's talents, experience, and resources, it extends to one's character, fashion or mode of operation, quality, and style. In other words, this order is inclusive of every relationship and every endeavour that is employed in one's life and that extends to the workplace environment. Workplace behaviour ethics are not compartmentalized but in fact must be, across the board, consistent behaviour that is the hallmark of a person's total life.

*Between law and religion*

I describe my work as filling a middle ground. On the one hand there is the law, which deals with crime and punishment. On the other there is religion, which deals with virtue and sin. Organizational ethics sits in between it goes well beyond the law, and links to the personal beliefs of employees, but its focus is the corporation ,association or government department. Such groups of people must work together to achieve common goals, while also striving to do the right thing in a complex, diverse world.

What I actually do is to help management and employees recognize moral dilemmas in decision-making, and provide ways for these to be discussed and resolved. I also try to strengthen common understanding of ethical norms that apply to modern corporate life. My brand of organizational ethics actually deals much more with creating and maintaining a healthy corporate culture than with exploring philosophical ethics applied to business. However, you will always discover that most problems occuring in the workplace could have been avoided if as a child the person was thought simple values.

*Values*

Organizational values often include such traditional virtues as trust, loyalty and commitment, honesty and respect for one another, and avoiding conflicts of interest. Values may also include newer elements such as innovation, teamwork, customer focus and continuous improvement. Or the more professionally minded people, these are ten cardinal workplace ethics that cut across all institutions. They are simple but relevant as it could undoubtedly cost some their jobs. Our children pass on values we parents pass on to them .If we fail to do this then they have no yardstick to measure there actions by.

*Guardrails for Good social conduct we could pass on.*

*1.Attendance*: Attend class, arrives/leaves on time, notifies instructor in advance of planned absences and makes up assignments punctuality.

*2.Character*: Display loyalty, honesty, trustworthiness, reliability, dependability, initiative, self-discipline and self-responsibility.

*3.Teamwork*: Respect the rights of others, is a team player, is cooperative, be assertive,display a customer service attitude; seek opportunities for continuous learning; and display mannerly behaviour.

*4.Appearance*: Displays appropriate dress, grooming, hygiene, and etiquette.

*5.Attitude:* Always demonstrate a positive attitude, appear self-confident and has realistic expectations of self.

*6.Productivity*: Follow safety practices ,conserve materials, keeps work area neat and clean and follow directions and procedures.

*7.Organizational Skills*: Manifests skill in personal management, time management, prioritizing, flexibility, stress management, and dealing with change.

*8.Communication*: Displays appropriate non-verbal and verbal skills.

*9.Cooperation:* Display leadership skills , appropriately handle criticism and complaints , demonstrate problem-solving capability, maintain appropriate relationships with supervisors and peers and follows chain of command.

*10. Respect:* Deal appropriately with cultural/racial diversity and do not engage in harassment of any kind.

### *Window of thoughts*

I walked into a room full of ten year old pupils at the learning centre I was assigned to teach a catch up class for the upcoming eleven-plus exams. I observed that only two out of fourteen students that were there even muttered a hello. Was it me ?Was it my clothes or didn't it occur to them that they should?I was keen to find out.

I decided to share my thoughts during lunchtime with a colleague who had been teaching Mathematics at the centre for years and to my dismay she said;

*"As long as they behave well and listen in class who cares if they answer or say hello!"*

Her mate Crystal however was on my side as she had experienced similar cold stares from her pupils too.

*"It's appalling but you'll get use to it soon she consoled me."*

So have you experienced cold stares from youngsters when you walk into a room , bus or a class?

Kaycee was born and raised in a military environment by a very Edwardian father and Victorian mother. Manners and etiquette were the order of the day, particularly regarding the relationships between children and adults. He spent most of his summers with his father's parents. They had come to Texas, as children, from Virginia. Though they came from families of some means. Those means soon dried up in the on-again off-again farming environment of Texas. By his day, meager was a very polite way to describe their economic situation. Through it all, however, they still had their education and manners.

Kaycees grandfather always stood when his grandmother entered the room or sat at the table. He only yelled when trying to get someone's attention from across the pasture. When guests were at the house, they were always introduced, even if they were then dismissed from the room or not part of the conversation. Kaycee attributes his strong moral foundation has kept him principled through hard times and when he was at cross roads between making a bad moral call.

Today, we see a gross violation of general manners and behaviour in the young people across the world . Simple things like acknowledging the presence of an adult (or even another child) entering the room or even looking others in the eye is lacking. Proper introductions are seldom made. Conversation is a lost art. The joy of sharing a meal is a rarity.

So who is to blame for this breakdown of common-sense principles?

There is no specific place to lay blame. The deterioration has occurred over a couple of generations. The many young couples raising children in the world today were not exposed to many of these things themselves and if they were they did not understand them at all.

It seems a bit archaic to many but there is much to learn from past generations. I recently reread *"George Washington's Civility"*. It is a bit dated in the details but the concepts are timeless. The first six follow as an example of it's contents:

1. Every action done in company ought to be with some sign of respect to those that are present.

2. When in company, put not your hands to any part of the body not usually discovered.

3. Show nothing to your friend that may affright him.

4 In the presence of others, sing not to yourself with a humming voice, or drum with your fingers or feet.

5. If you cough, sneeze, sigh, or yawn, do it not loud but privately, and speak not in your yawning, but put your handkerchief or hand before your face and turn aside.

6. Sleep not when others speak; sit not when others stand; speak not when you should hold your peace; walk not on when others stop.

A change in culture has to start somewhere. The best first place is within the walls of our own homes. The television, ipods, cell phones and video-games provide a whole new set of potential interferences in the daily manner and attitude of our homes. They all have there place, but they must be accompanied by rules of good civil behaviour. Human interaction needs to be moved to a higher priority. The bottom line is respect, not only for others but for ones self.

### *Troy's story*

Troy is a volunteer parent that went with a group of boys for a scout's outing.

*"This really came home to me a few weeks ago* "said Troy

*"I was bringing some of the boys and their gear home from one of those cold winter scout camps. At each house, I got out of the van, helped the boys unload their gear and said goodbye. Not once that day did I hear a "thank you" for driving them home, or even for coming with them on the outing. It was just a "bye" or no acknowledgement at all."*

## Why Children Need Manners

I suspect that all of us have had the experience of being mortified at our children's questionable manners at one time or another. They often seem to breach etiquette standards, and usually at the worst possible moment (like in front of your boss, grandma and grandpa or the minister). But embarrassment of the parents is just one reason why children need to exhibit manners. Other important reasons include:

*It demonstrates respect.* Mutual respect forms the foundation of many important relationships in life, and children who don't use socially acceptable manners convey a lack of respect.

*It makes children likeable.* Granted, not all children are motivated by social acceptance; in fact, some relish in destroying it. But for the most part, children want to be accepted and liked; displaying good manners is almost always a positive impression and invites people to be polite and respectful in return.

## Why Children Don't Have Good Manners

There are a variety of reasons why children act in an ill-mannered way. Some reasons have to do with how they were raised; some are the result of changing societal norms.

*Today's Parents Encourage Openness.* For the most part, the days of "don't speak until spoken to" and "be seen and not heard" for children are long gone. Those of us raised in such restrictive environments have swung the pendulum to greater openness and expression in our children. The rule has become that a child may express their feelings whenever they feel a need. However, we need to find ways to help children respect the needs of others while still expressing their own needs.

*Popular Culture Rewards Disrespect.* It doesn't take very keen observation to know that it has become popular to be ill-mannered. Looking at some of the popular characters for children in recent years (think Beavis and Butthead or the Simpsons), one can see that being rude and disrespectful has become cool.

*Real Life Role Models.* If my children are any indicator, the public behaviour of athletes, entertainers and even adult family members can have a huge impact. For my youngest daughter, a huge Hannah Montana fan, if Myle Cyrus does it, it must be okay. We have all seen the influence of pop stars like Britney Spears on the way young girls want to dress. It is a major challenge to overcome the negative influence of role models who often have boorish behaviour as their stock in trade.

Understanding the whys surrounding bad manners and knowing how it has become fashionable to behave rudely, what do we do about it in our own families? What are some specific steps we can take to teach proper social behaviour?

*Clean Up Our Own Acts.* I know this is a tough one, but what message do we as fathers send with our own behaviour? I have had to catch myself on more than one occasion as I experience a little road rage ("What a moron!") or frustration with an umpire or a referee at a sports game ("If that guy had one more eye, he'd be a Cyclops!"). Or even worse, when I am preoccupied around the house and perhaps bump into a family member without apologizing, I send a message of disrespect. Even the liberal use of "pleases" and "thank you" when asking my children to do something would go a long way.

*Start Them Young.* For those of us who have young children still at home, try reinforcing proper manners when the kids are still impressionable. When you have company at home, prime your child about what it takes to be a good host, and reinforce the positive behaviour when they say please, thank you and act politely.

*Apply the Golden Rule.* When your child is treated insensitively by others in a social setting, ask them later how they felt and the impression that they had of the offending party. Maybe they were snubbed at a party, or someone interrupted their conversation with one of their own. Then remind them gently that we should think of others' feelings and that this would be a good reminder of how they should treat others.

Children learn by both precept and example. We have to teach politeness, respect, and manners, but we owe our children a good example as well. By exemplifying respect and kindness in our own lives, and by reinforcing good behaviour, we can win the battle we are waging with popular culture.

# Chapter Five

## Do manners really matter?

Who really cares if a child behaves badly?Will society be better off if people are more considerate of each other?Transport for London (TFL)surely thinks so.

This London transport network in charge of trains, trams, buses and tubes in London had started a massive campaign tagged *"Together for London"*.

Transport for London (TFL) campaign aims to encourage commuters to be more considerate to one another when using public transport in London.

The campaign includes poster activity at bus and tube stations that will run for six months. The campaign features five characters called 'The Londoners' who make pledges ranging from ;

*'I will offer my seat' and 'I will not play my music out loud' and 'I will try to remember what it is like to be 14 again'.*

The Mayor of London at the time of the campaign , Ken Livingstone, said: "We can all behave thoughtlessly sometimes, often without meaning to. This campaign simply suggests we think about the affect of our behaviour on other passengers. We all share London's buses and Tube so a little thought for one another can make all of our journeys more enjoyable and less stressful."

### Seven tips for teaching good manners

- *Use positive reinforcement.* When children show good manners, tell them they're being great. "By far the best strategy is to catch kids being good. When a child is being considerate, give them praise and explain why you're doing it," says Dr Donnelly. "Shaming children doesn't help them develop morals or good self-esteem."

- *Instruct in small doses and do it as part of normal life*. Don't make it into a lesson. Work on one skill at a time, like how to answer the phone or how to use cutlery.

- *If kids do something thoughtless or rude, don't overreact* but explain what they've done wrong and how to do it right.

- *Set a good example.* If they catch you showing bad manners, admit it, then talk about other ways you could have handled the situation better.

- Remember that while young children will defer to you in social situations, later they turn to their peers to see how to behave. That's why it's important to teach them courteous behaviour as preschoolers and to keep it up at home.

- If you're going on a visit or out for a special occasion — say to a restaurant tell your children ahead of time what to expect and how you'd like them to behave.

- Emphasize the idea that it's good to think of others and that you should treat other people the way you would like to be treated.

The essence of good manners is showing consideration to other people, whether it's waiting your turn at a bus stop, letting someone else have the last biscuit or asking a stranger who's fallen over if they're all right.

It's easy enough to get a preschooler to say "please" and "thank you" (if they don't say it, they don't get want they want), but older children and teenagers also need consistent guidance from their parents on the appropriate way to behave.

Dr Donnelly says that talking and engaging with your children is the very best way to teach them.

*"Really young children do what they're told because the parents have the power. But when kids start to develop a mind of their own, say around age eight right through adolescence, parents really need to demonstrate how you deal with these complicated grey areas in social interaction."*

He recommends that by age seven and eight, you should be talking to your children about how things went in the day especially things that went wrong and how they and their friends reacted. Together you can work through what might be the best response to a problem.

*"This fosters moral development in a better way than just teaching them rules. You foster a process of the child working out what the civil thing is to do. You let the child work it out rather than just imposing rules — the more rules you impose, the more rules the adolescent has to rebel against."*

*"At the same time they have to know when to say 'that's not okay with me' and how to talk about being disappointed with someone else's behaviour. They have to learn how to do that in a well-mannered way,"* he says.

**Then there is television.**

*"I believe that television is worst of all in encouraging young people to behave badly. Every night there is violence, there is sex, there is bad language,"* says June Dally-Watkins.

The explosion in swearing on TV has many parents alarmed. Dr Donnelly suggests you counter TV's influence by pointing out that the box is not reality, that they can't use it to decide how to behave in real life.

Bad manners are the biggest problem facing our society, according to a study. Spitting and swearing are most unpopular manifestations of this, along with not saying please or thank you, and pushing in that order. Parents are largely to blame for the declining standards, according to the survey for an I TV programme.

Good manners are a thing of the past. According to a study, bad manners are one of the biggest problems facing our society. An even higher percentage, 86 per cent, agreed that Britons have become ruder over the last ten years. Ninety per cent of those questioned blamed the decline in standards on the example offered by parents. Just under three quarters said manners should be taught as part of the school curriculum.

The survey was carried out for the ITV1 Tonight programme "Bad Manners Britain".

Researchers also toured London with the British Transport Police and found many adults are just as impolite as the children most commonly blamed.

British Transport Police Sergeant Wendy Coad said;

*"I've had as many adults, if not more adults, be rude to me than school children."*

The top ten examples of bad manners, in order of rudeness, according to the survey were: Spitting, swearing, queue jumping/pushing in, not saying please or thank you, playing loud music in a public space, belching in public, speaking loudly on a mobile phone, inconsiderate driving, not giving a seat up for a pregnant woman, and not holding the door for the person behind.

What I have never but never understood is why people lack the most basic of manners. Manners don't cost anything at all, there is no charge for exercising them, they are free and frequently they yield an enormous return.

What does it cost anyone to say "Hello, how are you?", to smile, to exchange a pleasantry, to say "thank you", to stand aside to allow a woman out the door first, to hold a door open, to help someone pick up something, to assist people looking at maps?Society has broken down so much, the adage be your neighbours keeper no longer applies to most people.

**Jane's story**

Jane was in what used to be the local mall and I was checking out some shoes when she happened to look down. Under her right foot was a £50 bill and around her left foot were another four (4) £50 dollar bills or £250 in all. She stooped over to pick them up and at that moment the woman who ran customer service came by. Jane asked her ;

*"Do you know anyone that has reported that they lost money?"*

She said *"No"*.

Jane told her she had just picked up £250 in £50 bills. She looked at Jane and said nothing. The cashier then said ;

*"I think I may know who lost it since she just left here and she is a friend. I gave my number to the woman in charge of customer service, got the telephone number of the said woman and called the woman the cashier thought may have lost it. After I told her where to claim her money she hung up. She never even said thank you! Would you? I would, to say the least. If people sometimes wonder about the function of manners remember this story. All I wanted was "thank you".* Some people just do not know any better so they pass on the same to their children and onto the next generation.

Manners are the veneer of Civilization the polish that helps things function, the proof that we are civilized.

Parents that do not instruct their children in proper manners are bringing up children that will be rude and impolite to the world. If they later engage in female abuse or sexual harassment the parents should not be surprised. Manners are what make interpersonal relations pleasant and comfortable.

The lack of manners is far more noticeable than having good manners! If you have good manners you may not stand out in a crowd, but if you are a boor you stand out like a damaged thumb.


*Wise sayings;*

*1.Do It Yourself*

This is the most obvious tip, if you want your kids to eat dinner without putting their elbows on the table, then don't do it yourself!

*2. Many Small Talks*

I think that sitting down to have 'the manner talk' doesn't really work. You are better off teaching one or two things at a time as they come up.

*3. Be Careful of Friends*

Your teen might be great around you, but as soon as they get around a certain burpy, cursing friend their flatulence level goes from 0 to 60. You cannot forbade your kid from hanging out with them, but you can make them aware of how people treat this kid differently because of the way he acts (maybe teachers do not like his manners or at birthday parties other parents see him/her as rude).

*4. Don't Make a Stink*

One of the biggest pitfalls is that parents make a huge deal about manners. I am not saying you should not emphasize good etiquette, but when parents fight with kids about elbows, it makes the kids want to break the rule just because it makes you angry. Pick your battles, and light pushing is better than hardcore nagging.

## 5. *Lots of Praise*

We love to be praised! When we do it right, tell us–lots!

## 6. *Get Someone They Admire*

My parents gave me tons of advice when I was younger. I really do not remember any of it. Yet, I do remember every single thing my dance teacher or older cousin said to me during our once a year lunches. Get someone they admire to stress good manners and etiquette so they listen with new ears.

# Chapter Six

## Hegais prescription (For Christians)

This chapter's theme is based on what I call Hegais prescription which is from my favourite scripture in the bible.

**Esther 2:15**

*"Now when the turn of Esther the daughter of Abihail, the uncle of Mordecai,who had taken her for his daughter, was come to go in unto the King , she required nothing but what Hegai the kings chamberlain, the keeper of the women appointed. And Esther obtained favour in the sight of all of them that looked upon them. "*

The above speaks of Esther humbling herself to the tutelage of Hegai, the king's chamberlain. She was not the most beautiful of all the girls brought to the palace but she made a choice to listen to the wisdom of Hegai .Think of it, who else knew what the king liked but his chamberlain who saw and served him everyday for years. He knew exactly what the king would like, his favourite colours, the kind of perfume that attracted him, all the things he wanted to see in his Queen -Hegai knew. That's the privileged information Esther had and adhered to which made her eventually queen.

Taking a prescription takes respect and faith. It also takes a determination to have a meaningful result. The bible is the perfect prescription book for everything we are dealing with and here are a few tips and biblical backings to all the gibberish called etiquettes, manners and common sense we have been dealing with and the exciting thing about this particular kind of prescription is that the trend is constant and never fades. It cuts across generations and is applicable to cross cultures which is great!

You know manners always had some moral justification, something that made you feel hmm!" I'm doing the right thing or mumble to yourself, how could I have done that?"

For me, etiquettes is based on the golden rule;

*"Do unto others as you would have them do unto you."*

Courtesy, politeness and consideration for others is something that cuts across all cultures and indeed most religions. This however, sometimes take sacrifices as T. Emerson said *"Good manners are made up of petty sacrifices".*

Lets look at some etiquette tips and their biblical references that back it up.

### Good work ethics

The idea here is one of a position of responsibility and of submission to authority. 1Corithians4:2

*"Now it is required that those who have been given a trust must prove faithful"*
*"And in the same way, you masters must treat your slaves right. Don't threaten them; remember, you both have the same Master in heaven, and he has no favourites"*

### Do everything in moderation;

Live a simple life

1 Corinthians 10:31

*"Whatever you eat or drink or whatever you do, you must do all for the glory of God"*

### Have good listening skills;

Don't interrupt people in their speech especially when they are slow speakers.

Proverbs 17:27

*"He that hath knowledge spareth his words: and a man of understanding is of an excellent spirit. "*

Proverbs 18:13

*"He that answereth a matter before he heareth it, it is folly and shame unto him."*

James 1:19

*"Wherefore, my beloved brethren, let every man be swift to hear, slow to speak, slow to wrath:"*


### Do not believe everything you hear;

Never give your judgement to any matter until you hear both sides.

*Proverbs 14:15*

*"The simple believeth every word: but the prudent man looketh well to his going."*

*1Timothy 5:19*

*"Against an elder receive not an accusation, but before two or three witnesses."*

### Watch what you say:

Avoid speaking without thinking. It could bring you trouble .

Mathew12:37

*"For by thy words thou shalt be justified, and by thy words thou shalt be condemned."*

Proverbs 14:7

*"Go from the presence of a foolish man, when thou perceivest not in him the lips of knowledge".*

Proverbs 21:23

*"Whoso keepeth his mouth and his tongue keepeth his soul from troubles."*

### Respect elders

Do not talk back to your elders nor raise your voice at them.

1Timothy 5:1-2

*"Rebuke not an elder, but intreat him as a father; and the younger men as brethren;*

*The elder women as mothers; the younger as sisters, with all purity."*

Exodus 20:12

*"Honour thy father and thy mother: that thy days may be long upon the land which the LORD thy God giveth thee."*

**Do not exalt yourself;** *Try to be humble, don't stick out like a sore thumb.*

Luke 14:7-11

*"And he put forth a parable to those which were bidden, when he marked how they chose out the chief rooms; saying unto them.*

*When thou art bidden of any man to a wedding, sit not down in the highest room; lest a more honourable man than thou be bidden of him;*

*And he that bade thee and him come and say to thee, Give this man place; and thou begin with shame to take the lowest room.*

*But when thou art bidden, go and sit down in the lowest room; that when he that bade thee cometh, he may say unto thee, Friend, go up higher: then shalt thou have worship in the presence of them that sit at meat with thee.*

*For whosoever exalteth himself shall be abased; and he that humbleth himself shall be exalted.*

**Show loyalty and be truthful;** Be conscientious at all times and let people trust you.

Luke 16:12

*"And if ye have not been faithful in that which is another man's, who shall give you that which is your own?"*

**Be thoughtful and a good host;**

Being thoughtful , caring and considerate of a guest builds lasting friendships.

1Peter4:9

*"Use hospitality one to another without grudging."*

*1Peter 3:8*

*"Finally, be ye all of one mind, having compassion one of another, love as brethren, be pitiful, be courteous:*

**Dress appropriately;** *Wear what is comfortable but also presentable. Men will judge you by it.*

*1Samuel 16:7*

*"But the LORD said unto Samuel, Look not on his countenance, or on the height of his stature; because I have refused him: for the LORD seeth not as man seeth; for man looketh on the outward appearance, but the LORD looketh on the heart."*

Genesis 41:14

*"Then Pharaoh sent and called Joseph, and they brought him hastily out of the dungeon: and he shaved himself, and changed his raiment, and came in unto Pharaoh."*

Proverbs 7:10

*"And, behold, there met him a woman with the attire of an harlot, and subtle of heart."*

### AGURS ADVICE

Agur, an ancient sage who lived around the time of King Solomon, decried the lack of respect, purity, humility, and sensitivity that he saw among his own peers or the younger generation of his day. His observations are recorded in Proverbs 30:11-14:

*"There is a generation that curses its father,*
*And does not bless its mother.*
*There is a generation that is pure in its own eyes,*
*Yet is not washed from its filthiness.*
*There is a generation -- oh, how lofty are their eyes!*
*And their eyelids are lifted up [in arrogance].*
*There is a generation whose teeth are like swords,*
*And whose fangs are like knives,*
*To devour the poor from off the earth,*
*And the needy from among men "*

These proverbs condemn various forms of unwise behaviour and are connected with this common phrase which points to the fact that certain sins can permeate a whole society or time period." Indeed, we are this very day living "in the midst of a crooked and perverse generation, among whom [we as Christians] should shine as lights in the world" **(Phil. 2:15)**. Therefore, as Christians, we do not want to be characterized by the same traits as the unbelieving world. Paul writes in **Ephesians 5:3**,

*"Let it not even be named among you, as is fitting for saints."*

If you look at the Proverbs text, you'll note that the deplorable conduct of an ungodly generation includes:
- disrespect toward parents
- self-righteous attitude ("pure in its own eyes") that refuses to admit fault or failure
- mean-spirited and hurtful words toward others
- preoccupation with self that causes them to be insensitive to and even take advantage of the less fortunate.

Now let me ask you a question: *How many of your own kids struggle with these things?*

Let me answer that question for you: They *all* do. Why? Because it is their natural inclination as sinners! Yet by God's grace they can belong to "the generation of the upright" **(Psalm 112:2)**, who show their fear of God and faith in God through their conduct toward others!

***Table Manners;*** *How you behave at the table will show people how you really are. Always try to create a good impression, it also goes to show your whole family in a good light.*

Luke 14:7-14 (1-24)

*1 One Sabbath, when he went to dine at the house of a ruler of the Pharisees, they were watching him carefully. 2 And behold, there was a man before him*

who had dropsy. 3 And Jesus responded to the lawyers and Pharisees, saying, "Is it lawful to heal on the Sabbath, or not?" 4 But they remained silent. Then he took him and healed him and sent him away. 5 And he said to them, "Which of you, having a son or an ox that has fallen into a well on a Sabbath day, will not immediately pull him out?" 6 And they could not reply to these things.

7 Now he told a parable to those who were invited, when he noticed how they chose the places of honour, saying to them, 8 "When you are invited by someone to a wedding feast, do not sit down in a place of honour, lest someone more distinguished than you be invited by him, 9 and he who invited you both will come and say to you, 'Give your place to this person,' and then you will begin with shame to take the lowest place. 10 But when you are invited, go and sit in the lowest place, so that when your host comes he may say to you, 'Friend, move up higher.' Then you will be honoured in the presence of all who sit at table with you. 11 For everyone who exalts himself will be humbled, and he who humbles himself will be exalted."

12 He said also to the man who had invited him, "When you give a dinner or a banquet, do not invite your friends or your brothers or your relatives or rich neighbours, lest they also invite you in return and you be repaid. 13 But when you give a feast, invite the poor, the crippled, the lame, the blind, 14 and you will be blessed, because they cannot repay you. You will be repaid at the resurrection of the just."

15 When one of those who reclined at table with him heard these things, he said to him, "Blessed is everyone who will eat bread in the kingdom of God!" 16 But he said to him, "A man once gave a great banquet and invited many. 17 And at the time for the banquet he sent his servant to say to those who had been invited, 'Come, for everything is now ready.' 18 But they all alike began to make excuses. The first said to him, 'I have bought a field, and I must go out and see it. Please have me excused.' 19 And another said, 'I have bought five yoke of

*oxen, and I go to examine them. Please have me excused.' 20 And another said, 'I have married a wife, and therefore I cannot come.' 21 So the servant came and reported these things to his master. Then the master of the house became angry and said to his servant, 'Go out quickly to the streets and lanes of the city, and bring in the poor and crippled and blind and lame.' 22 And the servant said, 'Sir, what you commanded has been done, and still there is room.' 23 And the master said to the servant, 'Go out to the highways and hedges and compel people to come in, that my house may be filled. 24 For I tell you, none of those men who were invited shall taste my banquet.'"*

Who do you invite to a party? Who do you have over for dinner in your house?

These are important questions to Jesus, but we may not understand why. I hope I can give you a few hints as to why they are so essential. Often, when we don't understand someone, it isn't because we can't read his words, but because we have forgotten the wider context. What is the wider context?

### *Teaching the children is our responsibility*

Many of the values and concepts our children hear about at school, from playmates, or on television run counter to the life values we are trying to instill in them. We cannot control every input into their lives. But we can influence them at home.

Children hear a great deal of wrong information, for example, regarding moral issues. They hear of abortion, homosexuality, adultery, and situational ethics. They need our guidance to learn how to view these issues from a biblical perspective. When children reach adolescence and perhaps earlier,these topics should be discussed openly and often. They should always be discussed in light of the Scriptures.

In our family we plan to read and talk about portions of *"Whatever Happened to the Human Race"?* By Francis Schaeffer and C. Everett Kopeck. We feel it will give our children a healthy perspective for considering God's value for human life. It will open areas for discussion that might not otherwise come up. There are several Christian based resources that could be used as discussion sessions with your children.

Some of the negative influences draw our children away from God very subtly. We scarcely recognize what is happening until a large problem looms. If we consistently watch for such problems and, more importantly, offer continuous freedom to discuss them, we have a chance to redirect our children's thinking.

Many topics you discuss will fascinate your children to the point that they will want to continue talking about them at times other than devotions. This interest indicates the positive influence we can have with them.

A mother narrates her experience with this as follows;

I have three daughters in my family, and like most women they are interested in clothes and fashion. When my husband Jerry was travelling for a few weeks and our son was attending camp, we took a short course in fashion. We talked about matching colours, fabrics, and patterns. We cut "wish" wardrobes from magazines and modelled the ideal costume for one another.

Throughout the project I brought up the need for modesty in our dress. We don't want our girls to be puritanical, but we do emphasize that they represent Jesus Christ and that their attractiveness should be for his sake. We talked about the beauty that comes from within—being a lovely person in character as well as appearance. It was the most engaging conversation I had with my children for a long time. It opened doors to subsequent question and answer sessions with them thereafter.

Having a firm foundation on principles and time-tried truths like the ones mentioned above will endear children to behave better and make informed choices in life. Who cares more about us than the risen Christ , the one who took pain and grief for our sakes.

**Last Thoughts;**

My sincere hope is that you have been inspired to care more about the children God has put into our care and without a doubt would answer  if asked again "Who Cares? You would answer positively with an "I do."

*SETAPART*

*ANNUAL YOUTH*

*LEADERSHIP CONFERENCE*

Join us at the annual leadership conference this summer, learn tried truths of leadership and stewardship in a fun and warm atmosphere.

Register online at www.finishingtouchesgroup.org

**0r  Call + 44 (0)795 042 8753**

www.ingramcontent.com/pod-product-compliance
Lightning Source LLC
Chambersburg PA
CBHW060131050426
42448CB00010B/2070